Soulful
Baker

To my dear Mum
If only you knew xx

First published in 2017 by
Jacqui Small
An imprint of Quarto Publishing PLC
74–77 White Lion Street
London N1 9PF

Publisher: Jacqui Small
Commissioning Editor/Project Editor: Joanna Copestick
Managing Editor: Emma Heyworth-Dunn
Editor: Abi Waters
Photography: Lisa Linder
Senior Designer: Rachel Cross
Production: Maeve Healy

ISBN: 9 781 1 911127 24 6

A catalogue record for this book is available
from the British Library.

2019 2018 2017
10 9 8 7 6 5 4 3 2 1

Recipe Notes
• All eggs are medium unless otherwise specified.
• All milk is full-fat, but substituting with semi-skimmed
  would be fine.
• All butter is unsalted.
• I generally use silicone-coated non-stick baking paper.

Quarto is the authority on a wide range of topics.
Quarto educates, entertains and enriches the lives of
our readers – enthusiasts and lovers of hands-on living.
www.QuartoKnows.com

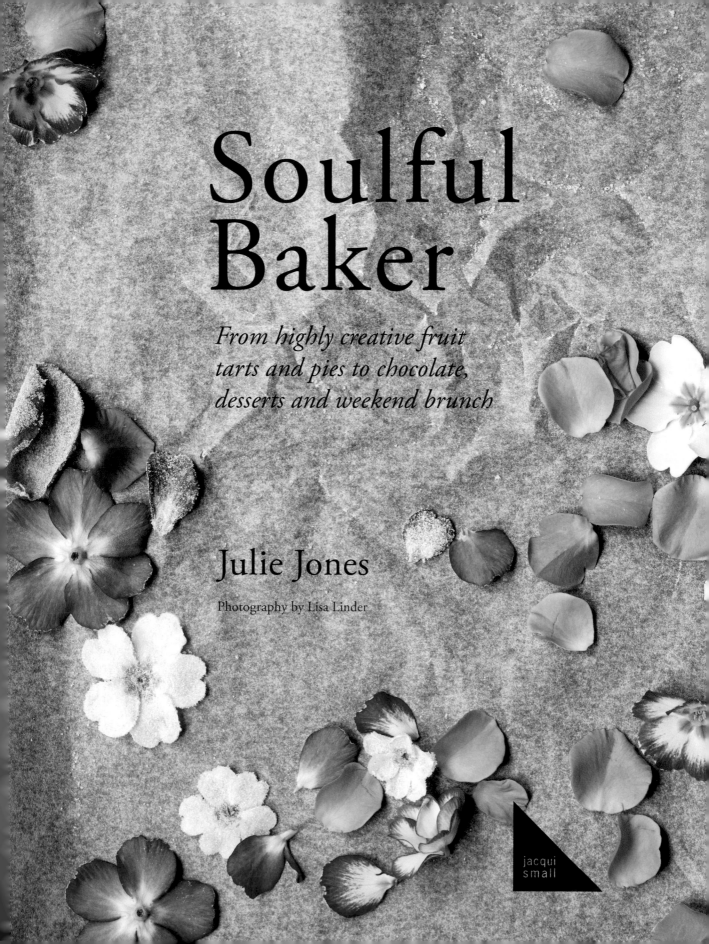

Soulful
Baker

*From highly creative fruit
tarts and pies to chocolate,
desserts and weekend brunch*

Julie Jones

Photography by Lisa Linder

jacqui
small

Contents

Introduction

For me, baking has always been associated with emotion. Those precious hours set aside to unwind and spend quality time preparing something with love and care. I was first introduced to baking when I was very small, stood upon a stool working alongside my Mother, her oversized apron folded in half and tied around my waist. I often think of her encouraging instructions and advice with affection, 'beat really fast – otherwise the batter will curdle'. No fancy or expensive equipment was used then, just a big ceramic bowl and a wooden spoon. Such happy days. Days I recreate with my own children now.

When my Mum became ill, it was baking that helped us to stay connected for as long as we possibly could. Her dementia made her very frightened of everyday activities and other people, her confusion and anxiety becoming so extreme that it was best to stay indoors. To pass the time we would bake together, making anything from a Victoria sponge to a Swiss roll. Those hours spent baking were like therapy, for both of us – her symptoms would ease dramatically and I would take comfort from having a sense of my real Mum back by my side. It was so incredibly sad to see her beautiful soul being taken away by this cruel disease, so heartbreaking it was to hear her ask me who I was. I knew that our time was limited, I knew that she would soon no longer know me at all.

I started to make a photographic record on Instagram of these precious hours of baking – something to look back upon and treasure. I started to use the space to express my emotions, my heartbreak at seeing my Mum slipping away from me. I soon connected with others that were going through similar, those who could empathize and sympathize, offering words of support and encouragement. In turn I was being told that my posts were inspiring to others and this also gave me great comfort. Something good was coming from all of the sadness. I shall be forever grateful to those connections and friends that I have made through Instagram.

After my Mum was taken into care, I turned to baking once more to help me through what I guess was grief. It's a strange thing to grieve for someone who is still alive. When the children were in bed I would immerse myself in creating pastries; never with a plan on how the finished bake would look, just going with the flow, being artistic and spontaneous, the creativity taking my mind away from losing my dear Mother. I continued to post my creations on Instagram and was bowled over by the kind words of support, the growing following and the daily encouragement that I was given to continue. It gave me great confidence to be open – to be me. I often receive pictures that I have been tagged in or sent – pictures of lovingly created pies or desserts that claim to have taken inspiration from my posts. I

can't tell you how much these messages and pictures mean to me; to know that I inspire others to bake and be creative really is very heart-warming indeed.

The recipes in this book range from the quick and easy to the more time-consuming and elaborate. Some were created within those quiet hours of mindful baking where I would have sudden ideas and flashes of inspiration; others are more nostalgic – my Mother's Carrot Cake (see page 55), my Nana's Bread and Butter Pudding (see page 138) and my interpretation of that wonderful Italian wedding cake (see page 143). If time is short, most of the longer recipes can be broken down into stages, the Charlotte Royale (see page 140) and Delizie al Limone (see page 143) being fine examples. Pastry cases (shells) can also be made in advance, ready to be filled and topped closer to the time you want to serve them. It is often the case for me to do so, juggling daily life and children, visiting my Mum and working means that I don't often have hours at any one time to concentrate on one thing alone. I often make a batch of pastry first thing in the morning, go through the rolling, resting and baking stages throughout the day when I get a spare 20 minutes here and there – then on to the filling and decorating in the evening when all is quiet and the day's stresses have eased. Being relaxed and being able to enjoy what you are doing will without doubt lead to a better result.

What is important, is to make these bakes your own, use these decorations as inspiration, as a starting point, but do go on to create your own patterns or finishes. It can be quite surprising what can appear in front of you when your creative side takes over! Be spontaneous, be unique, be authentic, be proud of what you are making and most importantly, bake with love in your heart.

xxxxx

Julie

FRUIT TARTS & PIES

Getting Pastry Right

To get the best possible results when making and baking your pastry it is always best to allow yourself plenty of time. The dough will be all the better for having a sufficient amount of time to chill and rest in the fridge in between the making, rolling and baking stages.

Making the Dough

When making the pastry, it is important not to over work the gluten once the milk and egg yolk have been added. It is essential to stop mixing the moment that a cohesive dough has formed after which it will then need time in the fridge to rest and chill sufficiently before being rolled. To aid the rolling process, flatten the pastry out by hand before it goes in to the fridge, pushing it down to form a large flat disc before wrapping it up in clingfilm (plastic wrap) and chilling for at least 30 minutes, but longer if you can.

Lining Tins (Pans)

When lining tart tins (pans), roll out a disc large enough to cover your tin (pan), allowing extra for an overhanging edge. When you roll out your pastry, place it between two sheets of non-stick baking paper. This will prevent you having to add extra flour. Push the pastry into the creases and sides of the tin (pan) using a little pastry wrapped in clingfilm (plastic wrap) does this job beautifully. If your tin (pan) has a fluted edge, use the handle of a wooden spoon (or similar) to push the dough into each groove, this will give your pastry case (shell) beautiful sides once baked. Leave enough pastry to completely overhang the edges – this will help to prevent the pastry case (shell) from shrinking during baking. Trim off the remainder, saving it in case you need to patch up any holes or cracks later on. Place the lined tin (pan) in the fridge for at least 30 minutes.

Blind Baking

I always blind bake my pastry cases (shells) to ensure the finished tart or pie will be crisp and fully cooked, top and bottom – there is nothing pleasant about under-cooked soggy pastry. Once the pastry has chilled sufficiently, prick the base gently all over with a fork. Take a piece of non-stick baking paper, a bit bigger than the lined tart tin (pan) and scrunch it up (this will help it fit to the corners properly once the baking beans have been added) and place on top of the pastry. Top

the paper with plenty of baking beans – it needs to be heavy to prevent the pastry from lifting during baking. I have seen bakers use everything from lentils to coins to do this, so if you don't have baking beans you could use these instead. Place on a baking sheet and bake in an oven preheated to 180°C fan/200°C/400°F/gas 6 for 15 minutes. Remove from the oven, carefully spoon out the baking beans and lift off the paper. The pastry will still look a little raw at this point, so return it to the oven for a further 5 minutes or until it has changed in appearance but is not yet golden.

Check to see if there are any holes or cracks in the pastry case (shell), and if there are, even tiny ones, fill them with some of the leftover pastry. Prepare an egg wash by mixing an egg yolk with a few drops of boiling water. Take the pastry out of the oven and brush the base and sides until it is evenly covered. Return to the oven for the final time, baking until a lovely golden colour has been achieved and the pastry seems crisp and cooked through – about 15 minutes. The overhanging pastry may look over cooked, but don't worry, this will be shaved off and discarded later.

Remove from the oven and leave to cool completely before trimming away the overhanging edge. I use a Swiss-style vegetable peeler for this, it is perfect for gently shaving away the excess pastry a layer at a time, leaving a neat finish without breaking the case (shell).

The pastry case (shell) is now ready for use. I would strongly recommend keeping the cooked case (shell) in the tart tin (pan) until it is either filled and served, or filled and re-baked to finish. An empty pastry case (shell) is a delicate thing indeed.

Sweet Shortcrust Pastry

This recipe makes enough pastry to line a 23cm (9 inch) round, 3cm (1¼ inches) deep loose-bottomed tart tin (pan). There will be leftover pastry for small decorations, however, if you are making a lattice pie or a fully covered pie, remember to make a double quantity. The amount you need depends on how intricate you become with your piecrust designs. Any leftover pastry can be wrapped in clingfilm (plastic wrap) and kept in the fridge for 3 days.

MAKES 465G (1LB)

230g (8oz/1¾ cups) plain
   (all-purpose) flour
125g (4½oz/½ cup/1⅛ sticks)
   unsalted butter, chilled and
   diced
50g (1¾oz/generous ⅓ cup)
   icing (powdered) sugar
zest of ½ lemon, zest of
   ¼ orange or 1 tsp vanilla
   bean paste (all optional)
1 egg yolk
2 tbsp milk

FOR EGG WASH
1 egg yolk

Place the flour and butter in the bowl of a free-standing mixer fitted with a paddle attachment and gently beat until the mixture resembles fine breadcrumbs. Add the icing (powdered) sugar and any flavourings, if using, and mix through. Add the egg yolk and the milk and mix until the dough only just comes together (over working the dough will result in a tough pastry). As soon as the dough starts to come together, stop the machine, turn out onto a work surface and bring the pastry together with your hands to form a ball. Push down, flattening the dough out to a thickness of about 1cm (½ inch) – this will ease the rolling out process later on. Wrap in clingfilm (plastic wrap) and rest in the fridge for at least 1 hour but preferably longer.

To line your tart tin (pan) successfully, refer to page 13 for some tips, if needed. Use as directed in the recipe and before placing in the oven apply an egg wash.

Decorative Techniques

If using the pastry for decorative purposes, roll out between two sheets of non-stick baking paper to 3mm (⅛ inch) thick. Shape or cut out as desired, giving the pastry a fine dusting of flour to make it easier to handle if needed. The recipe on page 14 moulds and cuts really well and you should have little problem in doing so. If you do find that it's very soft and difficult to work with, it may simply be too warm – the temperature of the kitchen and the baker's hands will invariably have an effect on the dough. Simply return it to the fridge to firm up, trying again after 30 minutes.

Top your pies with the pastry cut outs, lattices and decorations, securing the outer most placed pieces to the rim of the tart tin (pan) – press these pieces down, allowing the edge of the tin to cut away any excess pastry, securing them in place while doing so. Return to the fridge for at least 30 minutes before brushing with egg wash and baking. If you have created a pie crust that is quite intricate, it would be a shame to displace the carefully laid pieces by using a standard pastry brush. I use a small paintbrush for when my pie crusts need that little extra bit of care. To egg wash, use an egg yolk mixed with a few drops of freshly boiled water, then take time to brush every piece of pastry that is on show, creating a uniformed, neat covering. The finished result will be pleasing, golden and beautiful.

Frangipane

I adore the flavour of almonds in baking, the marriage between stone fruits and almonds being one of my all-time favourite combinations. Frangipane is a great way to bake with almonds, and is a perfect bed on which to nestle a variety of fruits, from plums to berries, prior to baking.

MAKES 600G (21OZ)
Enough to fill a 23cm (9 inch) tart

170g (6oz/¾ cup/1½ sticks) unsalted butter at room temperature
170g (6oz/generous ¾ cup) caster (superfine) sugar
170g (6oz) eggs (shelled and weighed), beaten
170g (6oz/1¾ cups) ground almonds (almond meal)

Place the butter and sugar in the bowl of a free-standing mixer fitted with the paddle attachment. Cream together until they are completely smooth and combined. With the mixer running, add a little of the egg and then a spoonful of the almonds. Repeat this sequence until all of the eggs and almonds have been added, giving a final mix until everything has blended together.

The frangipane is now ready to be used as per recipe instructions.

This can be made in advance, keeping it in the fridge in an airtight container until needed. Do bring it back to room temperature before using, as spreading hard frangipane over a delicate pastry case (shell) could cause it to break.

Apple Rose Tart

Apple roses burst onto social media a couple of years ago, adorning everything from tartlets to smoothie bowls. Upon seeing them, I and millions of others, set about re-creating our own versions. This apple tart is the outcome from that apple rose phenomenon, and I can only thank social media for the inspiration. I like to serve the tart warm with some vanilla poached apples and Crème Chantilly (see page 52).

SERVES 10–12

Use a 21cm (8½ inch) round, 3.5cm (1¼ inch) deep loose-bottomed tin (pan)

1 quantity of Sweet Shortcrust Pastry (see page 15)
1 quantity of Frangipane (see opposite)

APPLE ROSES
12 apples – try to use ones with a variety of coloured skins
3 lemons

Make, line and blind bake your pastry as instructed on pages 13–15, reserving some uncooked pastry to make decorative leaves later on. Leave the pastry case (shell) to cool completely, trim off any excess and leave the case (shell) in its tin (pan). Preheat the oven to 160°C fan/180°C/350°F/gas 4.

Make the frangipane by following the method given opposite and fill the prepared pastry case (shell) to three-quarters full. Keep any leftover frangipane for other uses.

Prepare the apple roses. Fill a large microwaveable bowl with cold water and squeeze in the juice of half a lemon. Core and halve 4 of the apples, then cut each half vertically into slices about 1mm thick. Use a mandolin if you have one but if not, try to slice the apples as finely as you can with a sharp knife. Submerge all of the cut apple slices in the acidulated water. Microwave the bowl of apples on full power for 5 minutes. This will soften the flesh so that the slices can be shaped easily. Test a slice by bending and rolling it between your fingers – if it cracks, microwave for a further 60 seconds or until the apple slices become soft and pliable. I have found that this time varies from apple to apple, so testing is vital. Drain off the water, submerge in cold acidulated water (using the juice of the other half of the lemon), and drain again.

Lay 8 of the apple slices on a clean tea towel in a neat row, overlapping each slice as you do so. Start to roll one end of the row and gently manipulate them into a complete roll, to resemble a rose. Place the apple rose in the frangipane, skin facing up, and spread out to get the effect of petals blooming. Repeat with the rest of the apples, preparing another batch of apple slices when needed. Continue until all of the frangipane layer has been covered with roses (you may not need all 12 of the apples). Gaps can be filled with single slices tightly rolled or swirled in between – it really is a case of being as artistic as you wish.

Roll out the reserved pastry. Cut out some leaves (or similar) by hand or with a cutter and lay them around the tart for added decoration.

Place the tart on a baking sheet and pop into the oven. Keep an eye on it during cooking as the fine slices of apple may catch before the tart is completely cooked. Placing a piece of foil over the tart towards the end of cooking should prevent this. After 45 minutes, insert a skewer into the middle of the tart and if it comes out clean, it is ready. If not, bake for a further 15 minutes and re-test. Remove from the oven, leaving the tart to cool before removing it from the tin (pan).

Classic Lemon Tart with Limoncello Strawberries

Lemon tart has to be one of my all-time favourite desserts. Smooth, creamy and zingy, it really is a perfect way to end a meal and can be enjoyed all year round. I like to make the first of the year in January, a refreshing move forward after the heaviness of Christmas, then when strawberries come into season, I macerate some in Limoncello and serve them alongside the tart with added texture in the form of meringue kisses (see page 26).

SERVES 10–12
Use a 23cm (9 inch) round, 3cm (1¼ inch) deep tin (pan)

1 quantity of Sweet
  Shortcrust Pastry
  (see page 15), with zest of ½
  lemon added with the icing
  (powdered) sugar

LEMON CUSTARD
6 eggs
240g (8½oz/scant 1¼ cups)
  caster (superfine) sugar
4 lemons
170ml (6fl oz/¾ cup) double
  (heavy) cream

STRAWBERRIES
300g (10½oz) strawberries,
  washed, hulled and cut into
  halves or quarters depending
  on size
2 tbsp caster (superfine) sugar
1 tbsp Limoncello (optional)

TO FINISH
Meringue Kisses (see page 26,
  optional)
basil leaves (optional)
edible flowers (optional)

Make, line and blind bake your pastry as instructed on page 13–15, reserving any leftover pastry for another use. Leave the pastry case (shell) to cool completely, trim off any excess and leave the case in its tin (pan).

Turn the oven down to 120°C fan/140°C/275°F/gas 1.

To make the lemon custard, crack the eggs into a large bowl and beat together using a fork, trying not to incorporate too much air while doing so. Add the sugar, zest of 1 of the lemons and juice of all 4, and finally the cream. Mix together thoroughly, then set aside for 10 minutes. If after this time any froth appears on the surface, spoon off and discard. Pass through a sieve, straining into a large jug, or something that can then be poured from easily.

Place the cooked tart (shell) still in its tin (pan) on a baking sheet and place on the middle shelf of the preheated oven. Pull the shelf out and carefully pour the lemon custard into the pastry case (shell), filling as close to the top as you can. If any bubbles rise to the surface, they can be easily popped by running the flame of a blow torch over the surface, but this isn't a necessity. Gently ease the shelf back into the oven, close the oven door and bake for 35 minutes. When ready, the tart should have a slight wobble towards the centre. If when gently shaken you feel it is still rippling towards the outer part of the tart, bake for a further 10 minutes and then re-check. The tart can go from being seemingly under cooked to being set solid in no time, so be vigilant. Once you are happy with the consistency, remove from the oven, leave the tart in its tin (pan) and leave to cool completely – it will continue to set further.

Place the strawberries in a bowl, add the sugar and Limoncello, if using, and leave the fruit to macerate until needed. When ready to serve, add a few freshly picked and torn basil leaves to the strawberries, and serve alongside a slice of the lemon tart, adding some Meringue Kisses for texture if you wish.

Zingy, fresh and utterly mouthwatering. One of my favourite desserts... ever.

Meringue Kisses

These little kisses are a great way to add extra pizzazz to a tart, cake or dessert, however they are equally as lovely on their own or perhaps dipped in chocolate. They would make a pretty gift too, wrapped up in cellophane bags and tied with colourful ribbons, or as an appealing alternative to the usual children's party favours.

MAKES 60–80 KISSES

1 lemon
100g (3½oz) egg whites
200g (7oz/1 cup) caster
  (superfine) sugar
food colouring gels (optional)
cocoa powder (optional)

Preheat the oven to 100°C fan/120°C/240°F/gas ¼–½. Before you start, it is important that your equipment is really clean and grease free. When satisfied, cut a wedge from the lemon and gently rub it all around the inside of the mixing bowl. Add the egg whites and whisk on a medium speed until they form soft peaks. Test to see if they are ready by tipping the bowl slightly – if the whites stay put, they are ready; if they slide, whisk for a minute longer and re-test.

Turn the mixer to a high speed and add the sugar to the egg whites, one spoonful at a time, allowing the sugar to be completely whisked through before adding the next spoonful. Repeat until all the sugar has been added. Continue whisking for 2 more minutes, until the meringue is stiff and glossy. Rub a little between 2 fingers, if grains of sugar can be felt, whisk for a minute or so longer and test again. When the meringue is smooth, the kisses are ready to be piped. Before piping, secure a piece of non-stick baking paper to a baking sheet by dabbing a little of the meringue under each corner.

If colouring the meringue, add a few drops of chosen food colouring at this stage, giving one final whisk through before adding it to a disposable piping (pastry) bag fitted with either a plain or star nozzle (tip). It is always best to go easy on the colouring as the colours can be surprisingly powerful.

To create an ombré effect, vary the depth of colour to a batch of meringue starting with just a few drops of colour. Pipe out some kisses, then return any meringue to the bowl and add a few more drops, piping and repeating until you have a varying hue of kisses. The same process can be used with cocoa powder to create varying shades of chocolate meringue.

To get the striped effect, food colouring gel is added to the inside of a disposable piping (pastry) bag. Squeeze some of the gel onto a plate and using a small paintbrush, brush stripes of colour down the length of the bag before filling it with meringue. Getting someone to hold the painted bag while you fill it is helpful so that the meringue falls into the bag vertically, keeping the stripes in place.

Pipe out as many kisses as you can, varying the sizes if so desired. It is also nice to use different nozzles (tips), if you have them. Bake for 1–2 hours or until crisp and cooked through. Check by lifting some off the paper, if they are completely dry underneath they are ready. Switch off the oven and leave the kisses inside until the oven cools completely. Store in airtight containers until needed.

Strawberry Firework Tart with Candied Pistachios & Chocolate Flowers

I'll never forget the first time I was taken to a 'pick your own' fruit farm, picking beautifully ripe strawberries that tasted unlike any others I'd ever eaten before. Every Summer I try to source the tastiest strawberries I can, and if I ever pass a 'pick your own' I just have to go in. Laden with the best strawberries I can find, I head home with only one thing on my mind… strawberry tart.

SERVES 10–12
Use a 23cm (9 inch) round, 3cm (1¼ inch) deep tin (pan)

1 quantity of Sweet
    Shortcrust Pastry
    (see page 15)
1 quantity of Crème Pâtissière
    (see page 39)

CANDIED PISTACHIOS
3 tbsp caster (superfine) sugar
100ml (3½fl oz/generous
    ⅓ cup) water
100g (3½oz) roasted unsalted
    pistachios, shelled

TO FINISH
750g (1lb 10oz) strawberries
Chocolate Flowers (see page
    31)

First make the pastry as instructed on page 15. While the pastry is resting in the fridge, make the Crème Pâtissière as instructed on page 39 and leave to cool completely. Line, blind bake, chill and trim the pastry case (shell), and leave in the tin (pan) as instructed on pages 13–15.

Lay the pistachios out on a clean tea towel. Fold the towel over and rub the nuts vigorously. This will take off any loose skins, exposing the lovely green flesh beneath. Pick out the nuts and set aside, discarding the skins.

To candy the pistachios, add the sugar to a small frying pan (skillet) and add the water. Stir to dissolve the sugar and heat through for 2–3 minutes until you have a syrupy consistency. Add the nuts to the pan and stir around to coat in the sugar syrup. Keep stirring until the sugar crystallizes. It will start to cling to the nuts, going lumpy and turning white. Pour the candied nuts onto non-stick baking paper or a silicone mat and leave to cool. Crush them to a fine crumb, using a rolling pin or similar.

Wash and prepare the strawberries, checking each berry as you do so. If any are bruised set aside for another use. Slice off the leaves being careful not to take too much of the flesh. Group the strawberries together in size order. Quarter each strawberry vertically, keeping them in the sized groups.

Give the Crème Pâtissière a good whisking so it is smooth and spoonable. Fill the pastry shell almost to the top, smoothing the surface with the back of a spoon. Place a little of the remaining Crème Pâtissière into a disposable piping (pastry) bag, and store any leftover in the fridge.

Start to assemble the strawberry quarters around the tart, starting on the outside and using the larger quarters first. Lay each quarter side by side, cut side up, until you complete the first circle. Repeat until you have covered the surface of the Crème Pâtissière, keeping similar-sized strawberry quarters next to each other. Pipe a little of the Crème Pâtissière around the edge of the tart and top with some of the crushed pistachios. Spoon a little of the crushed nuts in and around the tart too, then pipe some dots of Crème Pâtissière around the tart to create a contrast in colour. Finish with some chocolate decorations, such as flowers and butterflies (see page 31).

Chocolate Flowers

Piped chocolate decorations, or chocolate run outs, can be used to embellish any of your baked delights. You can create your own designs or use stencils to make anything from simple flowers such as these or more elaborate lace effect pieces that can go around a cake. The trick is to use a continuous flow of chocolate, the lines and swirls touching in places, joining to form one complete shape or pattern. I prefer to use acetate sheets for making my run outs, especially when creating lace collars, but non-stick baking paper will work too.

MAKES 20 FLOWERS

The amount of chocolate needed will depend on the design that you wish to pipe

25g (1oz) chocolate (milk, dark or white), broken into small pieces

Tape a sheet of acetate to your worktop. If using a template slide this underneath.

Set a large heatproof bowl over a pan of simmering water and add the chocolate. Leave to melt, stirring occasionally, until smooth and lump free.

Pour the melted chocolate into a disposable piping (pastry) bag and leave to cool for 1–2 minutes. Snip off the very tip of the bag (only a small hole is needed) and use the melted chocolate to draw simple flowers onto the acetate, trying to use a continual stream of the flowing chocolate and making sure to overlap the chocolate in places.

Transfer to the fridge to set for at least 15 minutes, but the setting time will depend on how finely the flowers have been piped.

When the chocolate is crisp, gently peel away from the acetate and use to decorate your chosen dessert, cake or tart.

You can experiment with other shapes too, such as a butterfly.

Deep-filled Apple Pie

Apple pie is one of those things that most people feel nostalgic about. I have many happy memories of eating apple pies drowned in custard round at my Nana's house. She was a great baker and made pastry often, with plate cakes, fruit pies and custard tarts amongst the highlights. Oh, and the fat squares – leftover pastry cut into thick portions that were later covered in butter! Homemade custard will always be my first choice to serve alongside apple pie, a recipe for which can be found on page 137. However, I know opinion will be divided on this one, so do go ahead and use your favourite accompaniment.

SERVES 8

Use a 23cm (9 inch) round, 3cm (1¼ inch) deep tart tin

PASTRY

345g (12oz/2½ cups) plain (all-purpose) flour

185g (6⅓oz/¾ cup/1½ sticks) unsalted butter, chilled and diced

75g (2¾oz/½ cup) icing (powdered) sugar

1 tsp vanilla bean paste (optional)

1½ egg yolks

3 tbsp milk

FILLING

4–8 cooking apples (depending on size)

100g (3½oz/½ cup/1 stick) unsalted butter

100g (3½oz/½ cup) soft light brown sugar

100ml (3½fl oz/generous ⅓ cup) water

1 lemon

¼ teaspoon ground allspice

½ teaspoon vanilla bean paste (optional)

TO FINISH

1 egg yolk, demerara sugar

Make the pastry as instructed on page 15, adding some vanilla as a flavouring if you want to. Using one half of the pastry, line the tart tin (pan), blind bake, cool and trim, leaving the cooked pastry in the tin (pan) to be filled and finished later as instructed on pages 13–15. Keep the remaining half of pastry in the fridge to be used for covering and decorating the pie.

Peel, halve and core the apples, then roughly chop into large chunks. Place the apples, butter, sugar, water, a squeeze of lemon juice and the allspice into a pan and gently cook for 10 minutes or until the apples are just starting to break down, the butter has melted and the sugar has dissolved. Gently mix to combine, taste and add some more sugar if the apples are too sharp. Transfer to a bowl, leaving the juices in the pan and leave to cool.

Add the vanilla to the reserved juices, if using, and bring to a simmer. Leave to bubble and reduce for 5–10 minutes, until thickened. Stir this back through the cooled apples and fill the blind baked pastry case (shell).

Remove the remaining pastry from the fridge and roll out between 2 sheets of non-stick baking paper to about 3mm (⅛ inch) thick. You could either cover the pie with one whole sheet of pastry, crimping the edges together and making a little hole in the middle for the steam to escape, or you could roll up your sleeves, relax and get creative! Use pastry cutters, braids, lattices, pastry flowers, balls or cut outs to decorate your pie as you wish. There are some tips on shaping and decoration on page 19. When you are happy with the decorative pie crust, transfer the pie to the fridge for at least 30 minutes.

Preheat the oven to 180°C fan/200°C/400°F/gas 6.

Add a few drops of boiling water to the egg yolk and gently brush over the pastry as evenly as you can – sometimes using your fingertip is easier for covering the more intricate parts. You can sprinkle over some demerara sugar if you wish (it gives a lovely crunch to the finished pie) or leave as it is. Bake for 30 minutes, remembering to keep an eye on the crust during baking as any smaller raised pieces of pastry may catch and burn easily. When golden, remove from the oven and serve either hot or cold with your favourite accompaniment.

Roasted Plum & Frangipane Tart

Plums and almonds are a match made in heaven. Don't be tempted to skip the gentle roasting of the plums, it will only result in the frangipane becoming less appetizing by doing so. The plums benefit from losing some of their juice prior to being baked, however, if you rescue the juices from the roasting tin (pan) and add them back to the tart after baking, none of that delicious plummy flavour will be lost.

SERVES 8–10
Use a 21cm (8½ inch) round, 3.5cm (1¼ inch) deep tart tin (pan)

1 quantity of Sweet
  Shortcrust Pastry
  (see page 15)
1 quantity of Frangipane
  (see page 20)

PLUMS
10 plums, halved and stoned
50g (1¾oz/3½ tablespoons)
  unsalted butter
demerara sugar, for sprinkling
thyme sprigs, leaves picked
  (optional)
50ml (2fl oz/scant ¼ cup)
  Kirsch (optional)

TO FINISH
2 tbsp apricot jam (jelly)
100ml (3½fl oz/generous
  ⅓ cup) water
flaked almonds, toasted
icing (powdered) sugar,
  for dusting

Make, line and blind bake your pastry as instructed on pages 13–15. Leave the pastry case (shell) to cool completely, trim off any excess and leave the case (shell) in its tin (pan).

Preheat the oven to 180°C fan/200°C/400°F/gas 6.

To roast the plums, lay the plum halves in an ovenproof dish, cut side up, and top each with a little knob of butter, a sprinkling of demerara sugar and a scattering of thyme leaves, if using. Finally, drizzle over the Kirsch, if using, and add 2 tablespoons of water to the bottom of the dish. Bake for 20 minutes, basting the plums halfway through. Remove from the oven and leave the fruit to cool. Once cooled, gently lift the plums out of the dish, drain on kitchen paper and set aside. Reserve any cooking juices for later.

Turn the oven down to 160°C fan/180°C/350°F/gas 4.

Make the Frangipane as instructed on page 20 and use it to fill the cooled pastry case (shell) three-quarters full. Arrange the plums neatly on top, pushing them down a little. Any leftover Frangipane can be stored in the fridge for another use.

Bake in the middle of the oven for 45–60 minutes. The Frangipane is cooked when a skewer inserted into the middle comes out clean. Check the tart after 45 minutes, but if needed continue to bake for a further 15 minutes. Do keep an eye on the top of the tart – it my start to catch before the Frangipane has cooked through. Placing a piece of foil over the top of the tart will help to prevent any burning. Once the tart is fully cooked remove from the oven and allow to cool a little before removing it from the tin (pan).

Meanwhile, tip the reserved roasted plum juice, the apricot jam (jelly) and water into a small pan. Bring to the boil, turn down to a simmer and reduce the liquid by half. Pass through a sieve, then brush the top of the tart with the hot jam (jelly) sauce. Scatter the top with toasted almonds and dust with icing (powdered) sugar. Serve warm with a good helping of thick Vanilla Cream (see page 52).

Rhubarb & Almond Galette

Galettes are a great baking fix when you are short on time. The frangipane only takes minutes to make and with no need to blind bake the pastry, a hot dessert could be on the table in under an hour. They can be as rustic as you please, with your chosen fruit piled into the centre in a carefree manner or, if a little more time is on your side, you can arrange the filling carefully to create a more eye-catching design. The fruits can be changed to suit the seasons – stone fruits, berries, apples and pears will all work well.

SERVES 8–10

PASTRY
1 quantity of Sweet
  Shortcrust Pastry
  (see page 15)

FRANGIPANE
100g (3½oz/½ cup/1 stick)
  unsalted butter at room
  temperature
100g (3½oz/½ cup) caster
  (superfine) sugar
100g (3½oz) eggs (shelled
  and weighed), beaten
100g (3½oz/1 cup) ground
  almonds (almond meal)

FILLING & TO FINISH
2–3 rhubarb stems
  (depending on the
  thickness)
3 tbsp demerara sugar
1 egg yolk
20g (¾oz/¼ cup) flaked
  almonds, toasted

First make the pastry as instructed on page 15. As there is no need to line a tin (pan) or blind bake, simply flatten the pastry and wrap in clingfilm (plastic wrap), leaving it to rest in the fridge until needed.

Make the frangipane as instructed on page 20.

Wash and slice the rhubarb stems in to equal-sized pieces and slice each piece in half to expose some of the lighter coloured flesh inside. This will give a contrast in colour to the rosy skin.

Remove the pastry from the fridge and roll it out between 2 sheets of non-stick baking paper to 3mm (⅛ inch) thick. Remove the top sheet of baking paper, then slide a baking sheet underneath the bottom.

Preheat the oven to 180°C fan/200°C/400°F/gas 6.

Add a generous amount of frangipane to the centre of the rolled pastry and spread it out evenly, leaving a 5cm (2 inch) border of pastry uncovered. Lay the prepared rhubarb onto the frangipane in neat rows, pressing each piece down as you do so – using the contrast of the inner flesh and the rosy skin to create a pattern, if you wish. When all of the frangipane has been covered, sprinkle over some of the demerara sugar. Lift the pastry border up and over the outer layers of the rhubarb, trimming the edges of the pastry prior to folding if a neater edge is desired. You can add more detailed decoration to the pastry border if liked.

Add a few drops of boiling water to the egg yolk and brush the top of the pastry border evenly. Sprinkle over the remaining demerara sugar and bake for about 30–40 minutes, until the pastry is golden and crisp, the rhubarb has softened and the frangipane is cooked through.

Scatter the toasted almonds over the finished galette. Serve warm or cold with vanilla ice cream, cream or crème fraîche.

Crème Patissière

Crème Patissière, or pastry cream, is something that I use in lots of different recipes throughout this book. In this chapter it is an essential part of the fruit tarts and later it is used in everything from the filling for the Choux Puffs (see page 72) to the Charlotte Royale (see page 140). It really is an indispensable component for lots of different baked treats and desserts, enhancing the flavour to suit the recipe.

MAKES 620G (22OZ)

6 egg yolks
125g (4½oz/scant ⅔ cup)
  caster (superfine) sugar
40g (1½oz/generous ¼ cup)
  plain (all-purpose) flour
500ml (18fl oz/generous
  2 cups) milk
1 tsp vanilla bean paste

Add the egg yolks and one-third of the sugar to a large bowl and whisk until the yolks are pale and have some volume. Add the flour and whisk to combine.

In a large pan, bring the milk, the remaining sugar and the vanilla to the boil, removing from the heat as soon as it does so. Pour a little of the hot milk over the egg yolks, whisking continuously, then add the remainder. Pour the custard back into the pan and bring to a gentle boil. Allow the custard to bubble and thicken for about 2 minutes, whisking throughout. Once thick and the taste of raw flour has gone, remove from the pan and place into a bowl, covering the surface with a layer of clingfilm (plastic wrap) before it cools, to prevent a skin from forming. Leave to cool completely, then keep it in the fridge until needed.

Use as directed in the recipe.

White Peach & Nectarine Tart

This tart is best made during the height of summer, when white peaches are fragrant and sweet and nectarines are at their very best. If summer is many months away and you would like to make a fruit tart, simply change the fruits to suit the seasons – plums and figs if in autumn or perhaps some lightly poached rhubarb if in spring. Many fruits will sit happily atop silky crème pâtissière and crisp pastry, so feel free to experiment.

SERVES 6
Use a 35 x 12cm (14 x 4½ inch) tart tin/pan (or a circular one if preferred)

1 quantity of Sweet Shortcrust Pastry (see page 15), with the zest of ½ a lemon added with the icing (powdered) sugar
1 quantity of Crème Pâtissière (see page 39)
1 egg yolk, for egg wash

TOPPING & DECORATION
3 yellow-fleshed nectarines (not overly ripe)
3 white-fleshed peaches (not overly ripe)
150g (5½oz) Lemon Curd (see page 155 or shop bought)

Make and bake the pastry, line and blind bake as instructed on pages 13–15. Leave the pastry case (shell) to cool completely, trim off any excess and leave the case (shell) in its tin (pan).

Preheat the oven to 180°C fan/200°C/400°F/gas 6.

Roll out any unused pastry to 3mm (⅛ inch) thick and cut out some decorative shapes using pastry cutters. Brush each with a little of the egg wash (the egg yolk mixed with a few drops of freshly boiled water) and bake for 10 minutes or until they are golden and crisp. Leave to cool, then set to one side until later.

Make the Crème Pâtissière as instructed on page 39 and leave to cool.

Wash and stone the fruit by running a sharp knife around the middle of each, going through the flesh until the knife hits the stone. Twist each half in opposite directions, pulling gently to ease the fruit from the stone. Some stone fruits do this with ease, some not so. If you can feel that the halves will not come away easily, simply cut the stone out instead, staying as close to the stone as possible, leaving the flesh intact. Finely slice across the width of each peach and nectarine half, then set to one side.

Spread an even layer of Lemon Curd over the base of the tart case (shell) saving a little to use on top. Put the remainder in a disposable piping (pastry) bag. Give the Crème Pâtissière a vigorous whisk, then spoon it over the Lemon Curd, filing the pastry case (shell) almost to the top. Place some extra Crème Pâtissière into another piping (pastry) bag.

Use 5–6 slices of the prepared fruit at a time and make roses out of the slices as with the apple roses on page 21. Place the fruit roses on top of the Crème Pâtisièrre with the skin facing upwards and spread out, tweaking the slices so that they resemble a blooming rose. Repeat until the cream has been completely covered. Small gaps can be filled with single slices tightly rolled or swirled and any remaining fruit can be cut and used for filling and added decoration.

To complete the tart, place the pre-cooked pastry shapes across the top of the tart in a decorative and eye-catching manner. Pipe little dots of the reserved Crème Pâtissière and Lemon Curd in and around to finish.

Strawberry & Cherry Pies

Making beautiful pies is something I enjoy doing very much indeed. I enjoy the creative freedom, getting lost in the design, going with the flow and seeing what happens. Ultimately, food is all about flavour and pleasure in eating, therefore no matter how pretty something is, it still has to be cooked properly. I always blind bake my pastry cases (shells) prior to filling and finishing, and I always make sure the finished pies are flavoursome and the pie crust is golden and crisp. Change the filling to suit the season or your craving, lots of fruits work well in pies. This recipe will make enough pastry and filling for three individual pies – so choose your favourite mini tins and get creative.

MAKES 3 INDIVIDUAL PIES
Using a selection of small tins such as a 10 x 9cm (4 x 3½ inch), 2cm (¾ inch) deep tin (pan) or a 12cm (5 inch), 2cm (¾ inch) deep round tin (pan)

1 quantity of Sweet Shortcrust Pastry (see page 15), with 1 tsp vanilla bean paste added with the icing (powdered) sugar if liked

FILLING
250g (9oz) strawberries, washed, hulled and quartered
250g (9oz) cherries, washed and stoned
4 tbsp caster (superfine) sugar
1 lemon

TO FINISH
1 egg yolk
demerara sugar, for sprinkling (optional)

Make the pastry as instructed on page 15, adding some vanilla as a flavouring if you want to. Using one half of the pastry, line your choice of tart tins (pans), blind bake, cool and trim as instructed on pages 13–15, leaving the cooked pastry in the tins (pans) to be filled and finished later. Keep the remaining pastry in the fridge to be used for covering and decorating the pies.

Place the prepared fruit in a bowl, sprinkle over the caster (superfine) sugar and add the juice from half of the lemon. Set aside to macerate for 30 minutes, tasting afterwards, adding more sugar or lemon juice if needed. Fill the cooked pastry cases (shells) with the macerated fruit.

Roll out the reserved pastry between 2 sheets of non-stick baking paper. How you decorate the pies is really up to you. The pies could either be covered with one whole sheet of pastry, crimping the edges together and making a little hole in the middle for the steam to escape, or get creative and make pretty pie crusts using pastry cutters, braids, lattices, pastry flowers, balls or cut-outs to decorate. There are some shaping and decorating techniques for inspiration on page 19.

When your crusts are finished, transfer the pies to the fridge for at least 30 minutes to rest and chill.

Preheat the oven to 180°C fan/200°C/400°F/gas 6.

Add a few drops of boiling water to a bowl containing the egg yolk and mix together well. Gently brush the egg wash over the pastry as evenly as you can – using a fingertip may be easier for the more intricate parts. Sprinkle over some demerara sugar and bake for about 20 minutes, keeping a close eye throughout, as any smaller raised pieces of pastry may catch and burn. Remove from the oven when golden and crisp all over. Serve either hot or cold with a generous helping of Crème Anglaise (see page 137), cream or ice cream as preferred.

CAKES, BAKES & TREATS

Successful Cake Baking

Baking cakes successfully isn't difficult and it needn't be daunting. Light and airy cakes, sponges and bakes are what we all seek as bakers. Armed with just a few tips and some knowledge to help you, your cakes, bakes and teatime treats can be magnificent every time.

Air

Depending on what is being baked, different techniques for incorporating air can give our bakes that lift we need. If you get as much air into your batter before it goes into the oven you are already on the way to a great bake. Throughout the book, various methods are used, but the secret to incorporating as much air as possible during these stages is knowing when to stop.

If using the creaming method (see pages 60, 64,68 and 114), beating the butter and sugar for long enough is what is key. When the method says 'light and fluffy' it really means that. When creamed for sufficient time, the butter and sugar change colour and the texture alters. If using a mixer, I suggest that you beat for at least 4 minutes on a high speed, doubling that time if beating by hand. If using the whisking method (see pages 140 and 143), eggs and sugar are whisked together until they become pale and increase in volume. Again, whisking for long enough is what is key, only stopping when a ribbon of the batter can be drawn into a figure of eight on top of the mixture, where it will stay in place when complete. I recommend whisking for 5 minutes on a medium speed when using a mixer and 10 minutes if whisking by hand.

Raising Agents

I was once given this tip from a pastry chef when gaining some work experience in a hotel in the Lake District. It is one I'd never heard before and neither have I seen it written in any baking book. He told me to always sieve the raising agent with the flour before re-sieving the combination into the other ingredients. The baking powder then becomes more evenly distributed, helping to give an even rise. This seemed to make perfect sense and I have always, and will always, do this when a recipe requires a raising agent.

Gluten

Care needs to be taken when flour is added to a cake batter. All of the other ingredients can be worked as long as necessary, but as soon as the flour goes in, mixing should be kept to an absolute minimum. This prevents the gluten from being over-worked prior to baking (exactly the opposite to what is required for bread making). Cakes should be light and crumbly and soft to the bite, breaking up easily when eaten. If you remember this next time you bake, I am sure your cakes will be lighter and more delicious for it.

Temperature

Knowing how your oven behaves for all of your cooking and baking is helpful. I know mine heats more on the right, browning everything much quicker on that side, therefore I know that my bakes benefit from a turn half way through. I also know that my internal oven temperature is dramatically different from that which the dial suggests. An oven thermometer is an essential bit of kit for bakers, so do get one if you don't have one already.

Time

Baking your cakes and sponges for long enough is crucial and although times are given in each method they can differ slightly from home to home. Ovens differ, tins (pans) differ through size or material, all factors that make a difference to baking time. Because of this it is also good to know how to tell when things are cooked through, double checking them before removing from the oven. For cakes, inserting a skewer into the centre is the norm; if it comes out clean, it is ready. A cooked cake will also release itself from the sides of the tin (pan), or when non-stick baking paper is used, the sponge and the paper separate with ease when ready. Check for movement, a gentle shake of the tin (pan) will help you to see if it has set. Colour and aroma will also change during cooking. Get to know the difference between the smells of a baking cake to that of the smells of a fully baked one.

Cook and bake with all of your senses in tune with one another and you will soon bake instinctively.

Vanilla Cream

This is barely a recipe at all, just a combination of two ingredients, but the crucial part is how the cream is whipped. The aim is to have soft, pillowy peaks that are velvety and spoonable yet whipped enough to be easily shaped either by piping or with a palette knife.

MAKES 300G (10½OZ)
Enough to layer a 3-tiered cake

300ml (10fl oz/1¼ cups)
  double (heavy) cream
1 tsp vanilla bean paste

Place the cream and vanilla in a large mixing bowl. Use a balloon whisk to whip the cream by hand, using a fast and assertive motion. As the cream starts to thicken, whisk gently until the right consistency has been achieved. If the cream does start to look lumpy and is clogging the whisk, it is likely that it has been over whipped. Adding a splash more cream and mixing it through should rescue it.

Alternatively, the vanilla could be stirred into the cream and served at pouring consistency.

Crème Chantilly

Crème Chantilly is essentially just whipped cream that has been sweetened with sugar, but it can also have a little alcohol or vanilla added to it. It can be used for many things – it is a great filler for cakes, delicious served with meringues and can transform fruit and pancakes into an indulgent and luxurious brunch.

MAKES 300G (10½OZ)

300ml (10fl oz/1¼ cups)
  double (heavy) cream
1 tbsp icing (powdered) sugar
splash of eau de vie (optional)

Place the cream in a large mixing bowl and sieve in the sugar. Whisk as you would with the vanilla cream (see above), making sure the cream isn't over worked. When starting to thicken, add a good splash of the eau de vie and continue to whisk until soft peaks form.

Cream Cheese Frosting

Cream cheese frosting will pretty much go with anything, from banana bread to chocolate cake, so do try it on other bakes too. It is important that the cream cheese and butter are at room temperature before making, so take both out of the fridge well in advance.

MAKES 470G (16½OZ)

200g (7oz) full-fat cream
  cheese
40g (1½oz/3tbsp) softened
  unsalted butter
250g (9oz/1¾ cups) icing
  (powdered) sugar
1 tsp vanilla bean paste

Add the cream cheese and butter to the bowl of a free-standing mixer and beat using the paddle attachment until well combined. Sieve in the sugar, add the vanilla and continue to beat until everything is smooth. If lumps are evident, pass through a sieve.

Tip: the frosting will be quite loose and easily poured or spread over a cake. If a thicker mix is desired, fold in 150ml (5fl oz/scant ⅔ cup) softly whipped cream to help pipe or spoon it into place.

My Mother's Carrot Cake

I love carrot cake; it is my absolute favourite – hands down. My Mum used to make this cake for me and I would know the moment I walked through the door if she had – the welcoming smell of warming spices filling the air. I've never found a better carrot cake than this one, and I've tried many, unable to resist a slice whenever or wherever I see some.

SERVES 6
Use two 16cm (6¼ inch)
round, 4cm (1½ inch) deep
cake tins (pans)

CAKE
225g (8oz) carrots, topped,
  peeled and grated
4 eggs
250g (9oz/1¼ cups) caster
  (superfine) sugar
250ml (9fl oz/generous
  1 cup) vegetable oil, plus
  extra for greasing
225g (8oz/1¾ cups) plain
  (all-purpose) flour
1½ tsp bicarbonate of
  (baking) soda
1½ tsp baking powder
1 tsp ground allspice
1 tsp ground cinnamon

TO FINISH
1 quantity Cream Cheese
  Frosting (see page 52)
180g (6½oz) toasted walnuts,
  to finish (optional)

Preheat the oven to 160°C fan/180°C/350°F/gas 4. Grease and line the cake tins (pans) with non-stick baking paper.

Give the grated carrots a firm squeeze to remove some of the moisture. Place in a large bowl along with the eggs, sugar and oil. Whisk everything together either by hand or in a mixer. Mix and sieve together all of the dry ingredients, then re-sift directly on top of the wet ingredients. Sieving twice will help to incorporate the raising agents equally throughout the flour, giving an even rise. Whisk to combine, stopping the moment that everything comes together, then split the batter equally between the prepared tins (pans).

Bake for 35 minutes, then insert a skewer into the centre of each cake to see if they are ready. If the skewer comes out clean, the cakes are cooked, if not, continue to bake for a further 10–15 minutes and then re-test. When fully baked, turn out onto a wire rack, remove the baking paper and leave to cool completely.

Make the Cream Cheese Frosting as instructed on page 52. Even off each cake, slicing through the very tops. Generously spread one with the cream cheese frosting, then place the other cake on top. Finish with more of the frosting and use the toasted walnuts to decorate, covering the sides and adding a few to the top. Fresh flowers can be used as added decoration if you like.

Chocolate & Vanilla Muddle Cake

I love getting my kids to bake with me – yes, it takes twice as long to tidy up but it's fun, especially when they rename your recipes. When I first made this cake with Myles, my youngest boy, he asked me what it was we were making. I told him that we were making a marble cake. Not having a vast vocabulary at this point he seemed to think about this for a little while, looked at the swirled batter and asked 'muddle cake?'. It did make me smile, and affectionately we have called our marble cakes 'muddle' cakes ever since.

The recipe below is for a chocolate and vanilla combination, but you could experiment with different colourings and flavourings to create many an eye-catching cake. It can be left un-iced and served with a cup of tea, or you could top with a rich chocolate ganache and turn it into a celebration cake. There are endless options. Once you know how to get those lovely stripes and swirls running through your cakes you will be sure to impress everyone who takes a slice, whatever the occasion.

SERVES 12–16

Use a 21cm (8¼ inch) square, 5cm (2 inch) deep cake tin (pan)

VANILLA BATTER
2 eggs
125g (4½oz/scant ⅔ cup) caster (superfine) sugar
100ml (3½fl oz/generous ⅓ cup) milk
125ml (4fl oz/½ cup) sunflower oil, plus extra for greasing
1 tsp vanilla bean paste
225g (8oz/1¾ cups) self-raising (self-rising) flour

CHOCOLATE BATTER
2 eggs
125g (4½oz/scant ⅔ cup) caster (superfine) sugar
120ml (4fl oz/½ cup) milk
125ml (4fl oz/½ cup) sunflower oil
225g (8oz/1¾ cups) self-raising (self-rising) flour
25g (1oz/¼ cup) cocoa powder

Preheat the oven to 180°C fan/200°C/400°F/gas 6. Grease and line the cake tin (pan) with non-stick baking paper.

To save a bit of washing up, make the vanilla batter first. Place all of the ingredients into the bowl of a free-standing mixer and fit the paddle attachment. Beat for 1 minute or until all of the ingredients are combined and the batter is smooth. Transfer to another bowl then mix together all of the ingredients for the chocolate batter in the same manner.

Start spooning the batters into the prepared tin (pan). Start off with whichever batter you reach for first (it doesn't matter one bit). Spoon 1 tablespoon of your chosen batter into the centre of the tin (pan) and then spoon 1 tablespoon of the other directly on top. Continue to do so until all of the batter has been used, alternating coloured bands of batter filling up the tin (pan). Run a skewer through the cake mix, creating swirls by alternating the direction in which you move the skewer.

Bake for 45–55 minutes or until the cake is completely cooked through. Check by inserting a skewer into the centre before removing it from the oven. The skewer will come out clean if the cake is ready. Turn out onto a wire rack and gently remove the baking paper. Leave to cool completely before slicing.

Classic Victoria Sponge with Strawberries & Cream

Victoria Sponge is a cake that holds a very special place in my heart. It was the first cake that my Mum ever taught me to make. It was a cake that we baked together during the earlier stages of her illness, and it was the first cake to feature on my Instagram page, which in turn reignited my passion for baking. I owe a lot to this humble cake, and for that reason I feel that it belongs within these pages. I have, however, given it a little twist, using different tastes of strawberry to make it my own.

SERVES 6
*Use two 16cm (6¼ inch)
round, 4cm (1½ inch) deep
cake tins (pans)*

STRAWBERRY COMPÔTE
250g (9oz) strawberries,
 washed, hulled and quartered
1 tbsp caster (superfine) sugar
1 point of a star anise
 (optional)
a few drops of lemon juice

CAKES
200g (7oz/generous ¾ cup/
 1¾ sticks) softened butter
200g (7oz/1 cup) caster
 (superfine) sugar
4 eggs
200g (7oz/1½ cups) self-
 raising (self-rising) flour
1 tsp baking powder
2 tbsp milk

TO FINISH
200ml (7fl oz/generous ¾
 cup) double (heavy) cream
50g (1¾oz/generous ⅓ cup)
 icing (powdered) sugar, plus
 extra for dusting
1 tsp vanilla bean paste
4 small strawberries
 crushed freeze-dried
 strawberries (optional)
Crystallized Flowers (see page
 126, optional)

Preheat the oven to 180°C fan/200°C/400°F/gas 6. Grease and line the cake tins (pans) with non-stick baking paper.

Place the strawberries in a bowl with the sugar, stirring to coat, then leave to one side to macerate.

Secure the paddle attachment to the mixer and add the butter and sugar to the bowl. Cream together for a few minutes until light and fluffy. Crack the eggs into a separate jug and beat together. With the mixer running, add a little of the egg at a time, letting it combine before adding some more – you may need to scrape down the sides of the bowl between each addition. Mix and sieve together the flour and the baking powder, then re-sieve into the mixing bowl (sieving twice will incorporate the baking powder more evenly). Add the milk, then beat together, stopping the very moment that everything combines.

Share the batter equally between the 2 prepared tins (pans), levelling out the surface of each with the back of a spoon. Bake for 40 minutes, checking after this time to see if the cakes are cooked. Insert a skewer into the centre of each, if the skewer comes out clean they are ready, if not return to the oven for a further 10 minutes and re-test. Once fully baked, turn out of the tins (pans), remove the baking paper and leave to cool completely on a wire rack.

Meanwhile, make the compôte. Tip the macerated strawberries and any juices into a small pan. Add 1 tablespoon of water and the star anise, if using, and bring to a simmer. Cook gently for 10 minutes or until the strawberries start to collapse and the juices turn syrupy. Add a few drops of lemon juice to sharpen, then transfer to a bowl and leave to cool.

Whip the cream, icing (powdered) sugar and vanilla into soft peaks, transferring to a disposable piping (pastry) bag if you have one. Cut the strawberries into small pieces and set both aside. Slice the top off each cake to even, then spoon the strawberry compôte and the syrupy juices over the surface of one. Top with the softly whipped cream and place the other cake on top. Cover with more cream, piping it on if you wish, add a sprinkling of freeze-dried berries and decorate with the fresh strawberry pieces and Crystallized Flowers, if using.

Financiers

Financiers are small French almond cakes traditionally baked in rectangular moulds. There is no need to go out and buy special tins, I use a mini muffin mould for mine. The shape doesn't affect the flavour of these delicious little cakes, but if you do ever happen to serve rounded ones to a Frenchman, perhaps it would be best to call them something else! These are wonderful served hot from the oven, but can be cooled and eaten later.

MAKES 18 FINANCIERS

*Use a tray with moulds
measuring 5 x 2.5cm
(2 x 1 inch) deep*

80g (3oz/⅓ cup/¾ stick)
  unsalted butter
3 egg whites
½ tsp vanilla bean paste
55g (1¾oz/generous ⅓ cup)
  plain (all-purpose) flour
130g (4½oz/generous 1 cup)
  icing (powdered) sugar
70g (2¾oz/¾ cup) ground
  almonds (almond meal)

TOPPING

seasonal berries or stone
  fruits, sliced, diced and
  stoned
flaked almonds (optional)
icing (powdered) sugar, for
  dusting (optional)

Preheat the oven to 180°C fan/200°C/400°F/gas 6.

Melt the butter in a pan and continue heating, allowing it to gently bubble until it turns a nutty brown colour. Do be careful not to let it burn. Cooking the butter this way will give a distinctive nutty flavour to the finished cakes. Once this has been achieved, take it off the heat, pass through a fine sieve, add the vanilla bean paste and leave to cool. It may also benefit from being passed through a sieve. Use a little of the butter to grease the moulds.

Separate the eggs, placing the egg whites into the bowl of your mixer, keeping the yolks for another recipe. Whisk the whites until they are frothy and have turned white but don't whisk them as much as you would when making a meringue. Stop just before they become thick and very white – they are whisked enough when individual bubbles are still visible.

Sieve the flour and icing (powdered) sugar into a bowl, add the almonds, making sure they are also lump free. Sprinkle everything onto the egg whites and using a large metal spoon or rubber spatula, fold together. Be gentle yet assertive, you want to retain as much air in the egg whites as possible. Once all of the dry ingredients have been mixed through, pour in the melted butter. Use the same folding action to mix until the butter is well combined. It may seem like the butter won't incorporate at first, but it will, just keep folding gently.

When the batter is ready, spoon into the greased moulds, filling each three-quarters full. Top each one with a suitable sized berry and/or a piece of fruit or two, then give each topping a gentle push down in to the mix. Alternatively, flaked almonds could be used.

Bake for about 15 minutes. The time may differ depending on the size of your moulds but you can check them by inserting a skewer into the centre of a financier – if it comes out clean, they are ready. I always remove one from its mould at this point, splitting it in half, just to make sure they're cooked through before removing the rest from the oven. Dust with icing (powdered) sugar once cooked if liked.

Celebration Cake

There will always be special days that call for a celebration cake, and if it is a homemade cake that has been decorated with care, everyone appreciates it that much more. This cake will adapt easily to any occasion, simply change the colours to suit and use appropriate sprinkles, candles and ribbons.

SERVES 10–12

Use three 19cm (7½ inch) round, 3cm (1¼ inch) deep cake tins (pans)

375g (13¼oz/1¾ cups/ 3½ sticks) unsalted butter, softened
375g (13¼oz/scant 2 cups) caster (superfine) sugar
9 eggs
450g (1lb/3½ cups) self-raising (self-rising) flour
½ tsp baking powder
100g (3½oz/1 cup) ground almonds (almond meal)
3 tbsp milk
food colouring gels (optional)

TO FINISH
250g (9oz/2 cups) fondant icing (powdered) sugar
200g (7oz) smooth strawberry jam/jelly (or other flavour of choice)
½ packet natural-coloured marzipan
cornflour (cornstarch), for dusting
a selection of colourful sprinkles
ribbons and candles

Preheat the oven to 160°C fan/180°C/350°F/gas 4. Grease and line the bottom of each cake tin (pan) with non-stick baking paper.

Place the butter and sugar in the bowl of a free-standing mixer. Attach the paddle and beat together for a few minutes until light in colour and fluffy in texture. Add 3 of the eggs, beat to combine, then add the remaining eggs, 3 at a time, beating well before each addition. It may be necessary to scrape the mixture down from the sides of the bowl.

Sieve together the flour and the baking powder and then sieve once more onto the beaten mixture. Pour in the almonds, add the milk and mix briefly, stopping the moment that everything comes together to form a smooth batter. Split equally between 3 bowls and, if using, add some food colouring to each batch of batter and mix well. Transfer each coloured batch into the prepared tins (pans) and level out with the back of a spoon or palette knife.

Bake for 30 minutes, testing before removing from the oven. Insert a skewer in to the middle of each – if the skewer comes out clean, they are ready. If needed, bake for a little longer then re-test. They may benefit from being turned around or the positions swapped over to ensure an even bake. When ready, remove from the oven, leave in the tins (pans) for 2 minutes, then turn out onto a wire rack, removing the pieces of baking paper. Leave to cool completely.

Prepare the fondant icing by adding small amounts of water to it at a time. A thick pourable consistency is what is needed so do go easy with each addition. When ready, cover with clingfilm (plastic wrap) and set to one side.

Place the jam (jelly) in a small pan and bring to the boil. Remove from the heat, pass through a sieve and return to the pan to be re-heated later.

Roll out the marzipan as thinly as possible between 2 sheets of baking paper. A sprinkling of cornflour (cornstarch) will also prevent any sticking. Leave the marzipan between the sheets of baking paper to prevent it from drying out while you prepare the cakes.

Slice any uneven tops from each cake, leaving each equal in depth. Turn the first cake over and spread a thin layer of jam (jelly) across the surface – reheating the jam (jelly) may be necessary. Place the next cake on top, its bottom facing

continued overleaf

upwards. Repeat with the jam (jelly), then add the final cake. Line the cakes up perfectly, then brush the surface and all around the sides of the cake with more jam (jelly).

Remove the top sheet of paper from the marzipan, invert on top of the cake and remove the other sheet of paper. Smooth the marzipan over the top of the cake and press down, securing it to the sides. Trim away any excess. It doesn't have to be perfect as it will be covered in fondant icing and sprinkles, but do try and make it as smooth as possible, especially on the top.

Lay a sheet of non-stick baking paper on the work surface and stand the wire rack and cake on top. Give the fondant a stir to loosen, adding a drop or two of water if the consistency has altered. Pour a generous amount of icing over the cake to cover. The excess will drip onto the paper underneath where it can be rescued and re-used for a second coating if needed.

Leave the cake to sit untouched for a few minutes, just to allow the excess fondant to fall down the sides. The fondant has to have stopped moving before the sprinkles are added, preventing them from slipping downwards too. Carefully remove the cake from the wire rack, give the rack a wash, then return the cake to it. Lay a clean sheet of paper underneath the wire rack to catch any sprinkles that fall during the next stage of decorating.

Mix together the selection of sprinkles and gently press them up against the sides of the cake – they will stick well to the icing as long as it doesn't dry out, so do move swiftly. Collect any fallen sprinkles from the paper underneath and re-use until the sides of the cake are completely covered. Decorate the top with extra decorations and candles if you wish and finish with a matching ribbon once the sprinkles have set in place.

Coffee & Walnut Mini Loaf Cakes

I'm a bit of a newbie to coffee, only starting to enjoy it fairly recently. My Mum loved coffee, she 'couldn't function' without her morning cup or three, or so she said. I would often try and join her in this morning ritual, but I just couldn't get used to it. Whether through age, changing tastes or persistence, I like coffee now, and fully understand her need for that morning boost! These little cakes are the perfect partner to that said cuppa but are equally as delicious with tea.

MAKES 8 MINI LOAF CAKES
Use individual tins (pans) measuring 9.5 x 6.8 x 4.2cm (3¾ x 2¾ x 1½ inches)

90g (3oz/scant 1 cup) walnuts, toasted and chopped
150g (5½oz/⅔ cup/1⅓ sticks) unsalted butter, softened, plus a little extra for greasing
150g (5½oz/¾ cup) caster (superfine) sugar
100ml (3½fl oz/generous ⅓ cup) milk
1 tbsp instant coffee granules
150g (5½oz) eggs (shelled weight)
150g (5½oz/generous 1 cup) self-raising (self-rising) flour
¼ tsp baking powder

COFFEE & COCOA ICINGS
2 tsp instant coffee granules
200g (7oz/1⅔ cups) fondant icing (powdered) sugar
2 tsp cocoa powder (optional)

DECORATIONS (OPTIONAL)
Chocolate Flowers (see page 31)
toasted walnuts, crushed

Preheat the oven to 180°C fan/200°C/400°F/gas 6. Lightly grease the tins (pans) with some butter, then place a strip of non-stick baking paper across the width of each, using enough paper to leave an overhanging edge on each side.

Toss the walnuts in a dry frying pan (skillet) set over a low heat and toast them for a few minutes to enhance their flavour and texture. Give the pan an occasional shake so they don't burn. When done, transfer to a plate and leave to cool before roughly chopping them into small pieces.

Place the butter and sugar in the bowl of a free-standing mixer fitted with the paddle attachment and beat both together for about 4 minutes, until light and fluffy. Use a few drops of the milk to dissolve the coffee granules, then add this to the rest of the milk, adding the eggs too. Give all a good whisk to combine, then with the mixer running, start to add the wet mixture a little at a time to the butter and sugar, allowing each addition to be incorporated before adding some more. Scraping down the sides of the bowl between each addition may be useful. Sieve the flour and baking powder into a bowl, then re-sift on to the other ingredients. Beat all together briefly, stopping the moment that everything comes together. Add the chopped nuts and after one final quick mix the batter is ready to be shared equally between each prepared tin (pan).

Place the tins (pans) on a baking sheet and bake in the middle of the oven, checking them after 20 minutes. Inserting a skewer into the centre of each cake is the easiest way to do this, if the skewer comes out clean, they are ready. If not, return to the oven for 5–10 more minutes. When fully baked, lift the cakes from the tins, remove the paper strips, then cool on a wire rack.

While the loaves are cooling, make the icing. Start by dissolving the coffee granules with a few drops of hot water. Add the coffee solution, a little at a time to 150g (5½oz/1¼ cups) of the sugar and mix through until a thick coating consistency has been achieved. If the icing is too runny, simply add more sugar and vice versa. If using the cocoa icing, add the cocoa powder to the remaining 50g (1¾oz/scant ½ cup) of fondant icing (powdered) sugar, then slowly add drops of water until the same consistency as the coffee icing has been achieved.

Once the cakes have cooled completely, decorate with the icings, adding some Chocolate Flowers (see page 31) or perhaps some toasted walnuts if preferred.

Dipped Lemon Madeleines

I like to rest my madeleine batter in the fridge for at least an hour before I want to bake them, so do give yourself a little time for this. Patience and care in baking will always end in a better batter! Madeleines are wonderful still hot from the oven, simply rolled in caster (superfine) sugar, but they can be eaten cooled and dipped into all kinds of sauces, curds or even melted chocolate. Here I have suggested dipping them into an icing made with fresh berry juice, then topped with some freeze-dried berries. These can be expensive to buy, but as you will only need a small handful, I suggest you simply pick some out of your breakfast cereals!

MAKES 24 MADELEINES
Use a 12-hole madeleine tin (pan)

130g (4½oz/generous ½ cup/1⅛ sticks) unsalted butter, plus extra for greasing
3 eggs
160g (5⅔oz/generous ¾ cup) caster (superfine) sugar, plus extra for rolling
grated zest of 1 lemon
140g (5oz/1 cup) plain (all-purpose) flour, plus extra for dusting
1 tsp baking powder
1 tbsp vegetable oil

BERRY ICING
50g (1¾oz) soft berries, such as raspberries, blackberries or blueberries
juice of 1 lemon
100g (3½oz/scant 1 cup) fondant icing (powdered) sugar
small handful of freeze-dried berries, crushed

Melt the butter gently in a small pan, then leave to cool. Add the eggs, sugar and lemon zest to the bowl of a free-standing mixer fitted with a whisk attachment. Whisk for about 5 minutes on a high speed, until the eggs are light and fluffy – or a good 10 minutes if doing so by hand. Sift the flour and baking powder together into a bowl, and then again into the bowl of your mixer. Sifting twice will help to incorporate the baking powder properly. Pour in the melted butter and the vegetable oil and fold everything together, using a gentle folding action. You want to retain as much of the lightness created during the whisking as possible.

Once the batter is smooth and combined, cover the bowl with clingfilm (plastic wrap) and rest in the fridge for at least 1 hour. In the meantime, grease the madeleine tin (pan) with some butter and sprinkle over some flour.

Preheat the oven to 190°C fan/210°C/413°F/gas 6–7.

Spoon a little of the cake batter into each mould – filling halfway up should be enough. It is difficult to give an exact amount so I suggest testing and baking one before filling the whole tray. Bake in the middle of the oven for about 8 minutes, until golden and risen, with the characteristic bump in the middle popping up during cooking.

Remove from the oven and either roll in caster (superfine) sugar while still hot, or if wanting to dip them in the fruity icing, cool on a wire rack first.

Re-grease and flour the madeleine tin (pan) and repeat the baking process until all of the batter has been used.

To make the icing, blitz your chosen soft berries in a food processor, then sieve out any little pips, retaining the juice. Add a few drops of lemon juice. Place the icing (powdered) sugar in a bowl and mix in the berry juice a little at a time until you have a thick dippable icing. Dip a corner of each madeleine into the fruity icing, then sprinkle with some crushed freeze-dried berries. Eat straightaway or leave to set if preferred.

Choux Puffs with Chocolate Cream

Choux pastry is lovely and light and is easier to make than many think. Piped into éclairs or profiteroles and filled with anything from whipped cream to flavoured crème pâtissière, choux pastries make for a great tea-time treat. The cooked pastry freezes really well and will only need to be thawed prior to filling.

MAKES 6 PUFFS

CHOUX PASTRY
150ml (5fl oz/scant ⅔ cup) water
100ml (3½fl oz/generous ⅓ cup) milk
100g (3½oz/½ cup/1 stick) unsalted butter
150g (5½oz/generous 1 cup) plain (all-purpose) flour
1 tsp caster (superfine) sugar
pinch of salt
4 eggs

FILLING
120g (4oz) dark chocolate, broken into small pieces
6 egg yolks
120g (4oz/scant ⅔ cup)caster (superfine) sugar
40g (1½oz/¼ cup) plain (all-purpose) flour
500ml (18fl oz/generous 2 cups) milk
½ tsp vanilla bean paste

DECORATING
icing (powdered) sugar, for dusting

Line a baking sheet with non-stick baking paper. The filling will need to be cool before using so I suggest that you make this first.

Place the chocolate in a heatproof bowl, sat above a pan of simmering water. When the chocolate has melted, remove from the heat and set aside.

Put the egg yolks and one-third of the sugar in a large bowl. Whisk the yolks and sugar until they are light and fluffy, then whisk in the flour.

Put the milk, remaining sugar and vanilla in a large pan and bring to the boil, removing from the heat as soon as it does so. Pour the hot milk onto the egg yolks in 3 stages, whisking as you do so. Return to the pan and bring to a gentle boil. Leave the custard to bubble and thicken for a few minutes, whisking throughout. Transfer to a bowl, add the melted chocolate and stir until fully incorporated. Cover the surface with a layer of clingfilm (plastic wrap) to prevent a skin from forming, then leave to cool completely, placing in the fridge until needed.

Preheat the oven to 200°C fan/220°C/425°F/gas 7.

Now, make the choux pastry. Put the water, milk and butter in a large pan and bring to the boil. When the butter has melted, add the flour, sugar and salt and beat until combined. Beat vigorously with a wooden spoon, or spatula until a stiff cohesive paste has formed, then remove from the heat to cool for 5 minutes.

Crack the eggs into a jug and lightly beat together. Add a little of the egg to the paste and beat until combined. Once the first addition of egg has been incorporated, add a little more, repeating until all of the eggs has been used. The paste should now be smooth, glossy and pipeable.

Transfer to a disposable piping (pastry) bag and snip off the end creating a 2cm (¾ inch) hole. Squeeze 6 domes of pastry approximately 6cm (2½ inches) wide and 2cm (¾ inch) high onto the lined baking sheet, flattening down any points with a wet finger. Transfer to the preheated oven, spraying the inside of the oven with water before closing the door. Bake for 15 minutes, until puffed and golden, then turn the oven down to 150°C fan/170°C/325°F/gas 3 and continue to bake for another 10 minutes until crisp.

Remove from the oven, make a small hole in the bottom of each choux puff, allowing the steam inside to escape. Cool completely on wire racks.

To assemble the puffs, spoon the chocolate choux cream into a disposable piping (pastry) bag fitted with a fluted nozzle (tip). Cut each choux bun in half horizontally, then pipe a generous amount of the chocolate cream into the bottom of each, return the top to each bun and finish with a dusting of icing (powdered) sugar.

Blackcurrant Scones

Scones seem to vary in appearance from one café to the next, some so tall that I can taste the baking powder just by looking at them. I prefer mine reasonably raised, soft to the bite and nothing but a pleasure to eat. I flavour mine with fresh blackcurrants rather than using the more traditional dried fruits, but you can use those just as successfully if you prefer. Lightness of touch is key too – over working the flour once the milk has been added will result in a heavy, tough scone. I like to serve these with my Lemon Curd (see page 155) and whipped cream, the lemon adding to the already tart blackcurrants. They do, however, work equally well with the more accustomed pairing of clotted cream and jam.

SERVES 10–12

500g (1lb 2oz/3¾ cups)
  self-raising (self-rising) flour,
  plus extra for dusting
1 tsp baking powder
110g (4oz/½ cup/1 stick)
  unsalted butter, chilled
  and cubed
110g (4oz/generous ½ cup)
  caster (superfine) sugar
120g (4½oz/1cup) frozen
  blackcurrants
220ml (7½fl oz/scant 1 cup)
  milk

TO FINISH
1 egg yolk
1 tbsp demerara sugar
  (optional)

Preheat the oven to 180°C fan/200°C/400°F/gas 6. Line a baking sheet with non-stick baking paper.

Sieve together the flour and baking powder, then re-sift into a bowl – sifting twice will incorporate the baking powder equally, giving an even rise. Rub in the butter – by hand or in a mixer fitted with the paddle attachment – until all of the butter is incorporated and the mixture resembles fine breadcrumbs.

Add the sugar, stirring through, then add the frozen blackcurrants – using frozen berries will make it easier to mix them into the scone dough without them bursting. Distribute the blackcurrants through the flour and add most of the milk. You may not need it all, so reserve a little at first. Bring the dough together, adding the rest of the milk if needed. Stop mixing the moment the dough starts to hold together.

Turn out onto a lightly floured surface, push the mixture together with your hands, then roll out to around 3cm (1¼ inch) thick. Cut out as many scones as you can using a 6cm (2½ inch) round cutter and bring the remaining dough together to re-cut. Place each scone onto the lined baking sheet and rest for at least 15 minutes.

Add a few drops of freshly boiled water to the egg yolk and whisk together. Brush the top of each scone with the egg wash and sprinkle over some demerara sugar, if using. Bake for about 15 minutes, or until golden, light and cooked through. Cool completely on wire racks before slicing in half and spreading with some of your favourite things.

Iced Lemon Biscuits (Cookies)

Iced biscuits (cookies) can be as elaborate and fun as you want them to be. There are so many different types of cookie cutters available that you could literally make biscuits (cookies) suitable for any occasion. They make beautiful gifts too, cut and decorated then wrapped to suit the person you have made them for. The options are limitless. I really enjoy getting creative when icing mine, never really having a plan, just going with the flow and letting the patterns emerge in the process. The kids love making these too; I just leave the icing in bowls for them, that way they can dip, spread and sprinkle their biscuits (cookies) to their heart's content. The biscuits (cookies) themselves are lovely and crisp and can be enjoyed un-iced too. You could swap the lemon zest for vanilla seeds or even add a drop or two of almond essence; enjoy them with a good cup of tea.

MAKES 20 BISCUITS (COOOKIES) DEPENDING ON CUTTERS USED
This will make about 20 biscuits (cookies), depending on the cutters used

90g (3oz/scant ½ cup/ 1 stick) unsalted butter, softened
80g (3oz/scant ½ cup) caster (superfine) sugar
20g (¾oz/4 tsp) granulated sugar
1 egg
200g (7oz/1½ cups) plain (all-purpose) flour, plus extra for dusting
¼ tsp baking powder
pinch of salt
grated zest of ½ lemon

ICING & DECORATING
250g (9oz/2 cups) royal icing (powdered) sugar, plus extra for adjusting consistency if needed
juice of half a lemon
water
selection of food colouring gels
sprinkles (optional)

Cream the butter and sugars together in a mixer fitted with a paddle attachment for at least 2 minutes, until light and fluffy. Add the egg and continue beating until combined. Sieve the dry ingredients together, then add them to the mixer, along with the lemon zest. Mix everything together until a cohesive dough has formed, stopping the moment everything comes together. Turn out onto a large sheet of clingfilm (plastic wrap), pushing together to form a ball. Flatten out with the palms of your hands, then wrap in the clingfilm (plastic wrap) and put in the fridge for at least an hour to chill and firm up a bit.

While the dough is chilling you can be prepare the royal icing. It is surprising how little liquid is required to make the icing (powdered) sugar pipeable so add cautiously, you can always add a drop more if needed. The consistency needs to be thick enough to hold when piping, but soft and fluid enough to work with. Place all of the sugar in a large bowl and add a good squeeze of lemon juice. Mix well and beat until the icing becomes more fluid, adding a little more lemon juice or water until you have the right consistency.

Split the icing into different bowls (depending on how many different colours you want to use) and add the different coloured gels to each one. They can be very bright so add delicately until the right hue has been achieved. Cover each bowl with clingfilm (plastic wrap) to prevent any drying out, or fill some plastic disposable piping (pastry) bags with the icings and secure.

Preheat the oven to 180°C fan/200°C/400°F/gas 6.

Line a baking sheet with non-stick baking paper.

Remove the dough from the fridge and place on a generously floured surface, dusting the surface of the biscuit (coookies) dough with flour too. Roll out to about 3mm (⅛ inch) thick, moving the dough around as you do so to make sure it hasn't stuck to the surface. Cut out biscuits (cookies) using your chosen cutters and lift each up with a palette knife and place on the baking sheet. Repeat until all of the dough has been used, leaving a space between each as they do expand a little when baking.

Bake for about 10 minutes. The baking time will vary depending on the size the biscuits (coookies) have been cut to, so just keep a close eye on them. When they are cooked, they will be golden all over, a little more so around the edges. Remove from the oven, leave to cool for a minute or two before transferring them to a wire rack. Leave to cool completely before decorating.

To decorate, snip off the very tip from each piping (pastry) bag and pipe a border around the edge of each biscuit (cookie). This will stop the rest of the icing from running off the edges and creates a neat edge. Using the same (or a different colour), squeeze out enough icing to cover the biscuits (cookies), helping the icing to reach the border with a cocktail stick or similar. Using different coloured icing, pipe out some decorative lines, dots, swirls or words and build the patterns and colours as you go. Be as creative and artistic as you wish, adding some sprinkles and decorations for extra décor if you want to. Leave the icing to set hard before eating.

Alternatively the icing could be spread across the biscuits with a palette knife, or the surface dipped in the icing to cover.

BREAD &
YEASTED DOUGH

Getting Dough Right

I haven't always had success with bread making, and it's only through practice and understanding that I now know what will make a great loaf. It's so easy to get disheartened when you have put so much time and effort into something and it just doesn't live up to your expectations. I guess it is essential to start with the basic breads – learn how to make the simple before starting on those that use different flours, need a starter or require a sourdough culture being fed and grown in the fridge for weeks prior to starting. I have included some great recipes in this chapter to get you started, ones that will hopefully ignite, or perhaps reignite, a love affair of bread making. Below are a few tips that I've discovered along the way, ones that I hope may be of some help to you.

Ingredients

Flour can vary so much; some seem to absorb liquid much easier than others, or you may need to use more flour than the recipe states as the dough seems sticky. What I suggest is to find a favourite brand or supplier and stick to it. You will learn just how much extra flour is needed, if any, and you will have consistent results.

Yeast. I use dried easy-bake yeast in each recipe I have given, mostly because fresh yeast isn't readily available where I live but also because I like having yeast to hand so I can make bread or other yeast products whenever I get the urge. I was always a believer that fresh must be best, and I am sure it may be, but I have seen the results that can be achieved with the dried version and I and anyone who has tried my breads have always enjoyed the end result. If you do prefer to use fresh, convert the quantities given using an online converter.

Patience

Patience and time in bread making are essential. It was one of my mistakes in the early days. I wasn't kneading for long enough, I wasn't letting the dough rise for long enough and I wasn't baking for long enough.

After making bread and yeasted doughs by hand so frequently over the years, and learning what a good dough should look and feel like, I now use a free-standing mixer to knead my dough. I have given instructions to do so in each recipe, but all can be successfully made by hand too. My suggestion if doing so would be to knead for double the time stated, and if you get to a point where you think you've kneaded for long enough but that time hasn't past, you haven't! Don't cut out time, be patient!

Be patient during the rising process, you can't rush it, it will rise in its own time. The temperature of the room plays a significant role. Do leave it until it is fully risen before moving onto the next stage and again bake for sufficient time.

Use your Senses

Watch and observe your dough transform while it is being kneaded – it is good to learn how it should look when it is ready. Whether making by hand or using a mixer, the dough will change, eventually forming a cohesive springy dough that will no longer stick to the work surface or the bowl in which it is being mixed. There are exceptions of course, some doughs are and should be sticky, but your recipe will advise if this is the case.

Feel and pinch the dough. Even though I now use a mixer to do the hard work for me, I always turn it out when ready and roll it under my hands, checking its spring and texture.

Smell. I am always aware of the smells changing in the kitchen when I am baking, I am tuned in without really thinking about it. I could almost rely upon my sense of smell to know when everything is ready, the altering aromas telling me the bread or cake is fully baked. This comes with repetition and practice, but try to make a mental note of the smells around you, especially during a successful bake, they will register in your subconscious and you will recognize them the next time around.

Trampoline Bread

This is such a great basic bread to master. I make this loaf every weekend, sometimes I leave it plain, sometimes I may add some olives, but my favourite flavouring of all is aniseed. The tiny seeds give the loaf a subtle fragrant undertone that works brilliantly. You may be wondering where trampolines fit into all of this. Well, they don't really – the bread only affectionately being named so by a friend after likening its bounce and springiness to that of a trampoline. A pleasing remark to the ears of a baker and a name that I have proudly given the recipe.

SERVES 6–8

Use a 21cm (8½ inch) round, 6cm (2½ inch) deep loose-bottomed non-stick cake tin (or a large loaf tin/pan)

500g (1lb 2oz/3⅔ cups) strong white bread flour, plus extra for dusting

2 tsp salt

7g (¼oz) sachet of easy-bake yeast

320ml (10½fl oz/generous 1⅓ cups) water

50ml (2fl oz/scant ¼ cup) olive oil, plus extra for oiling

1 tsp aniseed (optional)

Secure the dough hook to the mixer and place the flour, salt and yeast into the bowl, keeping the yeast apart. Warm the water and add the oil to it. With the mixer running, pour in the liquid, allowing the machine to mix and knead the dough for about 8 minutes, checking after this time. If the dough looks sticky and is still clinging to the sides of the bowl, add a dessertspoon of flour and knead for a further 2 minutes. The dough should be cohesive and smooth and should spring back if pinched between your fingers.

Lightly oil a large bowl and place the dough into it. Rub the top of the dough with a little olive oil, then cover the bowl tightly with clingfilm (plastic wrap). Leave the dough to rise in a warm place until doubled in size. This will take at least 1½ hours but sometimes longer, so do be patient.

Dust a work surface lightly with flour and ease the dough out of the bowl onto it. Handle the dough lightly and gently and spread it out a little – by no means do I mean flatten it. Sprinkle over the aniseed or other flavourings, if using, and fold the dough into itself and knead again, gently rolling it under your hands and bringing it into a ball shape.

Turn the dough over and placing a hand at each side, slide each in opposite directions, manipulating the dough into a neat round loaf. Place it in the baking tin (pan), cover loosely with clingfilm (plastic wrap) and leave to rise for about 1 hour, or until doubled in size.

Preheat the oven to 200°C fan/220°C/425°F/gas 7.

Bake in the middle of the preheated oven, spraying the oven with water before closing the door – this will create steam while the loaf is baking, giving a lovely crispy crust. Bake for 30 minutes, then remove the loaf from the tin, returning to the oven upside down. Bake for a further 10 minutes or so, until the loaf is golden, crisp, and sounds hollow when the bottom is tapped. Remove from the oven and leave to cool on a wire rack.

Grape & Thyme Focaccia

This bread is so good served alongside an oozing baked cheese, the sweetness of the grapes working perfectly. A great weekend supper to enjoy with your favourite bottle of red.

SERVES 6

Use a 21cm (8½ inch) square baking tin (pan)

375g (13oz/2⅔ cups) strong white bread flour

1 tsp salt

1 tbsp caster (superfine) sugar

7g (¼oz) sachet of easy-bake yeast

240ml (8fl oz/1 cup) tepid water

85ml (2¾fl oz/⅓ cup) olive oil, plus extra for oiling

100g (3½oz) green seedless grapes

100g (3½oz) red seedless grapes

2–3 thyme sprigs

sea salt flakes

Grease and line the tin (pan) with non-stick baking paper.

Secure the dough hook to the mixer and place the flour, salt, sugar and yeast in the bowl, keeping the yeast apart. Gently warm the water, add 35ml (1fl oz/ 2 tbsp) of the olive oil and pour both into the mixing bowl with the mixer set on a low-medium speed. Leave the machine to knead the dough for 8–10 minutes, or until a soft and cohesive dough has formed. If the dough looks sticky and is still clinging to the sides of the bowl, add a dessertspoon of flour and continue to knead for a further 2 minutes. When ready, place the dough in a lightly oiled bowl, covering it tightly with clingfilm (plastic wrap). Leave to rise in a warm place for around 1½ hours, or until doubled in size.

While the dough is rising, wash and cut each grape into 3 or 4 slices and set aside until needed.

After proving, transfer the dough to an oiled work surface, stretching and flattening it out to form a large rectangle. Rub a little olive oil over the surface and top half of the dough with a handful of the sliced grapes. Scatter over some picked thyme leaves and a generous sprinkling of sea salt.

Fold the dough in half, covering the grapes and seasoning, pressing down as you do so. Spread the dough again, then repeat with the oil and toppings, giving the dough a final fold. Place in the prepared tin (pan), coat the surface with the remaining oil and top with the remaining grapes and some more thyme leaves.

Cover the tin (pan) loosely with clingfilm (plastic wrap) and leave to double in size, filling the tin as it does so. This should take about an hour.

Preheat the oven to 200°C fan/220°C/425°F/gas 7.

Just before the focaccia goes into the oven, dip a finger into some olive oil and poke the surface of the dough a few times. Scatter over some more salt flakes and bake for 30–40 minutes until the bread is golden and cooked through. Remove from the tin (pan) and leave to cool on a wire rack.

Grissini

I love making grissini, as do the kids. We can happily sit for an hour or two, lots of different spices, herbs and pastes laid out before us. A sprinkling here, a pinch there, some left plain. Some will be spread with olive pastes and twisted into ropes, some will be rolled, some are left flat. There are no rules and that's why the kids enjoy it so much — nothing can go wrong. It's a great way to spend a rainy afternoon. I've given you some ideas for flavourings but do experiment with anything and everything you can find in your spice rack.

MAKES ABOUT 80 GRISSINI

280g (10oz/generous 2 cups) plain (all-purpose) flour
1 tsp salt
40g (1½oz/¼ cup) fine semolina
100g (3½oz/½ cup/1 stick) softened butter
50g (1¾oz/¼ cup) finely grated Parmesan
7g (¼oz) sachet of easy-bake yeast
200ml (7fl oz/generous ¾ cup) milk

SEASONING SUGGESTIONS
chilli flakes
fennel seeds
finely chopped rosemary
sesame seeds
cracked black pepper
sea salt flakes
black or green olives, stoned and blitzed to a paste and patted dry
tomato purée

Line 2 baking sheets with non-stick baking paper.

Secure the dough hook to the mixer and place the flour, salt and semolina into the bowl, along with the softened butter, Parmesan and yeast. Warm the milk until tepid and pour it into the bowl. Start to mix on a slow speed. The ingredients should come together easily, forming an oily looking dough. Leave the machine to knead the dough for 10 minutes or so. If after this time the dough seems too wet, add a sprinkling of semolina and knead for a few minutes more. Cover the bowl with clingfilm (plastic wrap) and let the dough rest and rise for an hour. Preheat the oven to 180°C fan/200°C/400°F/gas 6.

Split the dough into 4 equal-sized pieces and roll one of the pieces into a rectangle of about 30 x 20cm (12 x 8 inches).

FOR STRAIGHT CUT GRISSINI
Sprinkle over your choice of seasonings and cut into lengths about 1cm (½ inch) wide. Transfer to one of the baking sheets, lifting up each end carefully as you do so. Bake for about 10–15 minutes, turning halfway through. The time can vary depending on the width and thickness to which the grissini have been cut and rolled so do keep an eye on them. Remove from the oven and place on wire racks.

FOR TWISTED GRISSINI
Spread or sprinkle a thin layer of seasoning across the bottom half of the rolled dough, folding down the top half to cover. Press down slightly then re-roll, sandwiching the flavourings in the middle. Neaten up the edges with a cutting wheel or knife and cut into lengths about 1cm (½ inch) wide. Lift up each end and twist in opposite directions. The seasonings will show along the cut sides, especially if a paste or purée is used. Place on the baking sheet and bake as before. Because the twisted grissini are slightly thicker, they will take slightly longer to bake. Do keep a close eye on them as they can burn easily, especially at the ends.

Roll, flavour and shape the grissini until all of the dough has been used. Once all have been baked and have completely cooled, store in an airtight container.

Swedish Kanelbullar (Cinnamon Buns)

The smell that fills the kitchen when baking these bread buns is just heavenly, with the wonderful aroma of spices filling the air. I bake them in a muffin tray, so the butter cannot escape during baking, instead seeping back into the dough, but they can be left to have their second prove rested upon a lined baking sheet and baked on that if you don't have one.

MAKES 18

250ml (9fl oz/generous
  1 cup) warm milk
100g (3½oz/½ cup/1 stick)
  unsalted butter
500g (1lb 2oz/3⅔ cups)
  strong white bread flour,
  plus extra for dusting
1 tsp salt
50g (1¾oz/¼cup) caster
  (superfine) sugar
7g (¼oz) sachet of easy-bake
  yeast
1 egg
oil, for greasing

FILLING

30g (1¼oz/2 tbsp) caster
  (superfine) sugar
2 tsp ground cinnamon
1 tsp ground cardamom
75g (2¾oz/scant ⅓ cup/
  ¾ stick) unsalted butter,
  softened

GLAZE

1 egg yolk
2 tbsp milk
sugar nibs

Heat the milk and butter together in a small pan and remove from the heat once the butter has melted, then set to one side and allow to cool until tepid.

Secure the dough hook to the mixer and place the flour, salt, sugar and yeast in the bowl, keeping the yeast apart. With the mixer running, pour the liquid into the dry ingredients and crack in the egg. Leave the machine to knead the dough for about 8 minutes, after which the dough will be soft and a little sticky. If it looks and feels overly sticky and is still clinging to the sides of the bowl, add a few dessertspoons of flour, one at a time, kneading continuously until it is less so.

Lightly oil a large bowl and place the dough into it. Cover tightly with clingfilm (plastic wrap), then leave to rise for at least 1½ hours in a warm place, or until doubled in size.

To make the filling, beat the sugar and spices into the softened butter until evenly mixed, then set aside.

When the dough has doubled, transfer to a work surface that has been dusted with flour. Roll out to a large rectangle, measuring about 45 x 35cm (18 x 14 inches). Trim the edges to neaten, then spread the spiced butter over one half of the dough, working lengthwise. Fold the other half down, covering the filling, then press down to secure. Gently re-roll the rectangle, neatening any uneven edges as you go.

Use a sharp knife or cutting wheel to cut the dough into long strips about 1cm (½ inch) wide. Twist each strip to resemble a rope, then roll up and twist to form a knot, tucking the loose end underneath. Place each bun into a muffin tray (or on to a pre-lined baking sheet) and cover loosely with clingfilm (plastic wrap). Leave to rise for about 30–60 minutes in a warm place, or until doubled in size.

Preheat the oven to 200°C fan/220°C/425°F/gas 7.

Make the glaze by beating together the egg yolk and milk and brush each bun evenly. Sprinkle over the sugar nibs and bake for 12 minutes, or until beautifully golden and cooked through, testing one before removing them from the oven. Leave to cool upon wire racks before eating, if you can resist!

Hot Cross 'Hearts & Kisses' Buns

Hot cross buns don't only make an appearance at Easter time in my house. They are far too tasty to be only made once a year. I absolutely love the aroma of them baking, and the warming spices wafting through the kitchen is one of my favourite baking smells of all. I like to use allspice and cinnamon in mine, and add different dried fruits such as cranberries, golden raisins and blueberries, but do mix this up if you prefer. When served hot from the oven, spread with some good salted butter and a drizzle of honey, they really are wonderful. However, they are equally as delicious halved and toasted the next day… if they last that long.

MAKES 9

Use a 21cm (8½ inch) square high-sided baking tin (pan)

50g (1¾oz/3½ tbsp) unsalted butter, melted

350g (12oz/2½ cups) strong white bread flour

pinch of salt

35g (1¼oz/2 tbsp) caster (superfine) sugar

1 tsp ground allspice

½ tsp ground cinnamon

7g (¼oz) sachet of easy-bake yeast

140ml (4½fl oz/generous ½ cup) tepid water

1 egg

100g (3½oz) dried fruits – golden raisins, cranberries and blueberries or similar

oil, for greasing

SPICED GLAZE SYRUP

100ml (3½fl oz/generous ⅓ cup) water

2 tsp caster (superfine) sugar

pinch of allspice

CROSSING BATTER

50g (1¾oz/⅓ cup) strong bread flour

pinch of salt

20g (¾oz/1½ tbsp) unsalted butter, melted

80ml (2¾fl oz/scant ⅓ cup) water

Grease and line the baking tin (pan) with non-stick baking paper.

Gently melt the butter in a small pan then set aside, leaving to cool slightly. Secure the dough hook to the mixer and place the flour, salt, sugar, spices and yeast in the bowl, keeping the yeast apart. With the mixer running, pour in the warmed water and the egg and then the melted butter. Leave the machine to knead the dough for 8–10 minutes, after which the dough should look cohesive and smooth. If it does look sticky and is still clinging to the sides of the bowl, sprinkle in a dessertspoon of flour and mix for a further 2 minutes. Add the fruit to the bowl and knead for a further minute or two.

Lightly oil a large bowl and place the dough in it. Rub a small amount of oil over the top of the dough and cover the bowl tightly with clingfilm (plastic wrap). Leave to rise in a warm place until doubled in size – this will take at least 1½ hours, but sometimes longer so do be patient. Once the dough has risen, ease it out of the bowl onto a lightly floured surface and split the dough into 9 equal-sized pieces, weighing them if you want to be precise. Use a cupped hand to roll each piece into a ball. Place each bun into the baking tin (pan), leaving an equal-sized gap in between each one. Cover the tin lightly with clingfilm (plastic wrap) and leave to double in size until the buns are touching and filling the tin – this will take about an hour.

In the meantime, make the spiced glaze by heating everything in a saucepan until simmering. Set aside until needed.

Preheat the oven to 200°C fan/220°C/425°F/gas 7.

Make the crossing batter by whisking everything together in a bowl. Whisk vigorously to make sure it is lump free – if some lumps refuse to budge, push it through a sieve – the mixture will be very thick. Place this into a disposable piping (pastry) bag and once the buns are ready for the oven, snip off the tip and pipe out the hearts, crosses and kisses, or just the traditional crosses if preferred, over the top of each bun.

Bake for about 15 minutes, until the buns are plump and golden on both the tops and the bottoms. When ready, remove them from the oven and immediately brush over the spiced glaze. Take them out of the tin (pan), peel off the baking paper and set upon a wire rack.

Braided Challah

Braided Challah breads look so impressive – some of the more elaborate Challah loaves using as many as eight strands. Here I use four, which suits my braiding abilities just fine. Being a mum to three boys I've never had much practice – the only thing I get to plait is bread dough and pastry! This bread is soft and delicious simply spread with butter and honey for a comforting snack anytime of the day. Any leftovers would make great pain perdu (bread that is soaked in a sweetened egg and milk mixture, then fried) the next morning and it would work brilliantly in bread and butter pudding too.

SERVES 8

MAKES ONE LOAF

80g (2¾oz/⅓ cup/¾ stick)
  unsalted butter
500g (1lb 2oz/3⅔ cups)
  strong white bread flour
1 tsp salt
2 tbsp caster (superfine) sugar
7g (¼oz) sachet of easy-bake
  yeast
150ml (5fl oz/scant ⅔ cup)
  water
50ml (2fl oz/scant ¼cup)
  milk
2 eggs
oil, for greasing

GLAZE
1 egg yolk
1 tsp milk

TO FINISH
icing (powdered) sugar
  (optional)

Line a baking sheet with non-stick baking paper.

Melt the butter in a small pan and leave to cool until tepid. Secure the dough hook to the mixer and place the flour, salt, sugar and yeast into the bowl, keeping the yeast apart. Mix the water with the milk, then heat until lukewarm. With the mixer running, pour the warmed, milky liquid onto the dry ingredients, adding the eggs and the melted butter. Leave the machine to knead the dough for about 8 minutes until a smooth cohesive dough has formed.

Place the dough into a large lightly oiled bowl, then cover tightly with clingfilm (plastic wrap). Leave to rise in a warm place until doubled in size – usually 1½ hours but it could take longer depending on the environment.

Once the dough has risen, ease it out of the bowl and split the dough into 4 equal pieces – weighing them if you want to be precise. Roll the portions beneath your hands, shaping each into a long cylindrical strand measuring about 40cm (16 inches).

Lay the strands of dough vertically in front of you, securing the furthest end by firmly pushing and nipping the end of each strand together, then start to plait the dough. The easiest way (in my opinion) is to think of the 4 strands of dough as 2 pairs. Take the right side of each pair and cross it over the left, then cross the 2 strands that are in the middle, left over right. After each middle crossing, go back to looking at the 4 four strands as 2 pairs and repeat the process.

To get a neat finish, try not to pull and stretch the dough as you plait – it will cause weakness and may tear during the next rise. Instead, gently lift and place each strand close to the next to form a tight, neat plait. When the end of the plait is reached, shape the loaf into a ring, joining and pinching the dough together firmly. Slide the lined baking sheet underneath the bread and cover with lightly oiled clingfilm (plastic wrap). Leave to rise in a warm place for about an hour, or until doubled in size.

Preheat the oven to 190°C fan/210°C/413°F/gas 6–7.

Beat together the egg yolk and milk and brush the Challah ring evenly. Bake for 40 minutes, or until the loaf is golden and cooked through. Transfer to a wire rack and leave to cool before slicing.

Caramel Bread

This bread was born simply by my inherent need to use up leftovers. On this particular occasion, it was caramel sauce that had been left looming in the fridge after a dessert of churros a few nights before. After a bit of experimental baking the said sauce ended up layered between sheets of bread dough, which was then served in a pool of caramel custard. A definite case of food upcycling if there ever was. That said, please don't wait until you have leftover caramel sauce to try this recipe, make the sauce for it and enjoy.

SERVES 8
Use a 19cm (7½ inch) circular cake tin (pan)

2 x quantities of Salted Caramel (see page 120)
80g (2¾oz/⅓ cup/¾ stick) unsalted butter
500g (1lb 2oz/3⅔ cups) strong white bread flour
1 tsp salt
2 tbsp caster (superfine) sugar
7g (¼oz) sachet of easy-bake yeast
100ml (3½fl oz/generous ⅓ cup) milk
100ml (3½fl oz/generous ⅓ cup) water
2 eggs
oil, for greasing

GLAZE
1 egg yolk
1 tsp milk

Grease and line the cake tin (pan) with non-stick baking paper.

To make the Salted Caramel sauce, follow the method on page 120. Set aside to cool.

Now, make the bread. Melt the butter in a small pan and leave it to cool until tepid. Secure the dough hook to the mixer and place the flour, salt, sugar and yeast in the bowl, keeping the yeast apart. Combine the milk with the water and heat until lukewarm. With the mixer running, pour it into the bowl. Crack in the eggs and add the melted butter, mixing together to form a dough. Leave the machine to knead the dough for about 8 minutes, after which the dough should be cohesive and smooth. If the dough seems sticky and is still clinging to the sides of the bowl, add a dessertspoon of flour and knead for a further 2 minutes.

Place the dough into a large lightly oiled bowl and cover tightly with clingfilm (plastic wrap). Leave to rise in a warm place until doubled in size – usually 1½ hours, but possibly longer.

Once the dough has risen, ease it out of the bowl and split into 3 equal portions. Roll each piece of dough, as thinly as possible into a large circle. Cover 2 pieces of dough with a thin even layer of caramel sauce – reserving some for later. Stack one of the caramel-covered pieces directly on top of the other and top those with the plain piece. The edges of each layer won't meet exactly but this only adds to the charm once swirled.

Use a sharp knife or a pizza wheel to cut the layered dough into 8 strips – there is no need to be too precise or even. Roll up each strip and place into the tin (pan), flattest side down. Lay the 8 swirls around the tin, leaving a gap between each. Cover lightly with clingfilm (plastic wrap) and leave to rise in a warm place for about an hour, or until doubled in size.

Preheat the oven to 180°C fan/200°C/400°F/gas 6.

Make a glaze by beating together the egg yolk and the milk then brush it over the risen dough evenly. Bake for 40 minutes, or until the loaf is golden and cooked through. Remove from the tin (pan), peel off the baking paper and leave to cool a little before spooning or brushing over the remaining caramel sauce. This bread is best served oozingly warm.

Doughnuts

My kids love these, and since we don't really have many fried foods at home, I don't mind making them as a treat now and then. Personally, I prefer to simply roll mine through gently spiced sugar. The boys like theirs glazed and dotted with sprinkles, especially if they have decorated them themselves.

MAKES 16 DOUGHNUTS

You will need 16 pieces of non-stick paper cut to about 10cm (4 inches) square

50g (1¾oz/3½ tbsp) unsalted butter
150ml (5fl oz/scant ⅔ cup) milk
50ml (2fl oz/scant ¼ cup) water
400g (14oz/3 cups) strong white bread flour, plus extra for dusting
½ tsp salt
1 tbsp caster (superfine) sugar
7g (¼oz) sachet of easy-bake yeast
1 egg
1.5 litres (50fl oz/generous 6 cups) vegetable oil, for frying

GLAZE & TO FINISH
125g (4½oz/1 cup) fondant icing (powdered) sugar
125g (4½oz/1 cup) royal icing (powdered) sugar
food colouring gels
sprinkles

Gently warm the butter in a saucepan, once melted remove from the heat and leave to cool. Mix the milk and water together and heat until lukewarm. Secure the dough hook to your mixer and place the flour, salt, sugar and yeast into the bowl, keeping the yeast apart. With the mixer running, pour in the warmed liquid, add the egg and the cooled butter and work the dough for about 8 minutes. If after this time the dough looks sticky and is still clinging to the sides of the bowl, add an extra dessertspoon of flour and continue to knead for a further minute or two. The dough should be cohesive and smooth looking and should no longer stick to the bowl.

Lightly oil a large bowl, place the dough in it and cover tightly with clingfilm (plastic wrap). Leave the dough to rise in a warm place until doubled in size. The time will differ but it will certainly need a minimum of 1½ hours.

Once the dough has risen, ease it out of the bowl onto a lightly floured surface and roll out to 1cm (½ inch) thickness. Use a 7cm (2¾ inch) cutter to cut out as many doughnuts as you can. Re-form the dough, re-roll and cut out some more if you can. Use a smaller cutter – a 3cm (1¼ inch) one should be about right – to cut out the hole from the centre (but do keep the middle bits for smaller bite-size doughnuts!). Place each doughnut on a piece of the pre-cut baking paper and lay each side by side in a warm place and cover lightly with clingfilm (plastic wrap). Give the doughnuts about an hour to double in size.

Heat the oil to 180°C/350°F either in a deep fat fryer or a large heavy-based pan. If you don't have a thermometer, add a cube of dry bread to test the heat – if it turns golden within 30–60 seconds, the oil is ready. Fry the doughnuts in batches by lifting each (still on their paper) and placing, paper and all, carefully into the hot oil. Don't worry, the paper won't burn, it will just slip away from the doughnut a few seconds after they enter the oil, after which it can be removed with tongs and discarded. Dropping them into the oil this way will stop the doughnuts from being misshapen due to handling. Fry for 4–6 minutes, turning halfway through. The doughnuts should puff out and be lovely and golden. Remove from the oil with a slotted spoon and drain on kitchen paper. Leave to cool completely.

For the glaze, mix together the fondant and royal icing (powdered) sugars with a few drops of water – just a little at a time – until a thick pouring consistency has been achieved. Colour the icing if so desired, then dip each doughnut into the icing, allowing any excess to drip away. Decorate with sprinkles or sugar decorations to your heart's content, then allow to set before eating.

Chocolate Twist Loaf

This bread has been inspired by the traditional Jewish loaf, Babka. The beautiful twists and layers of chocolate create such a decorative finish, which is not only a pleasure to look at but it is a joy to eat too. Needless to say, the kids love this bread, as they do anything that contains chocolate spread!

MAKES 1 LOAF
Use a 900g (2lb) loaf tin (pan)

90g (3oz/scant ½ cup/¾
  stick)unsalted butter
375g (13oz/2⅔ cups) strong
  white bread flour
pinch of salt
30g (1¼oz/2 tbsp) caster
  (superfine) sugar
7g (¼oz) sachet of easy-bake
  yeast
120ml (4fl oz/½ cup) milk
100ml (3½fl oz/generous
  ⅓ cup) water
1 egg
oil, for greasing

FILLING
200g (7oz) chocolate hazelnut
  spread

SYRUP GLAZE
100ml (3½fl oz/generous
  ⅓ cup) water
50g (1¾oz/¼ cup) caster
  (superfine) sugar

Grease and line the loaf tin (pan) with non-stick baking paper.

Melt the butter in a small saucepan, then set aside to cool until tepid. Secure the dough hook to the mixer and place the flour, salt, sugar and yeast into the mixing bowl, keeping the yeast apart. Warm the milk and water until lukewarm, adding it to the bowl along with the egg and the melted butter. Leave the machine to mix, then knead the dough for about 8 minutes by which time the dough should be cohesive and smooth. If the dough is sticking to the sides of the bowl, sprinkle in a dessertspoon of flour and continue to knead for a few more minutes.

Lightly oil a large bowl and place the dough in it, covering the bowl tightly with clingfilm (plastic wrap). Leave the dough to rise and double in size for at least 1½ hours.

Roll the dough out into a rectangle measuring about 30 x 45cm (12 x 18 inches), positioning the rectangle so that the longest edge is closest to you. Cover the surface of the dough with a thin layer of chocolate spread. Roll the rectangle fairly tightly into a long cylindrical shape, finishing so that the seam is on the underside.

Run a sharp knife or cutting wheel down the middle of the rolled dough, leaving 2cm (¾ inch) intact at one end. Starting at this end, twist the 2 lengths together, placing one under and over the other, exposing the chocolatey layers giving a rope effect. Carefully lift the twisted bread into the lined loaf tin (pan), pushing it together a little if needed. Loosely cover with clingfilm (plastic wrap) and leave to rise in a warm place for an hour or so until doubled in size.

While the loaf is proving make the sugar glaze. Put the water and sugar in a small pan and bring to a simmer. Continue to simmer until the sugar has dissolved and the solution has reduced to a syrup. Remove from the heat and set aside.

Preheat the oven to 180°C fan/200°C/400°F/gas 6.

Bake the bread in the middle of the oven for 40 minutes, or until the bread is golden and cooked through. Remove from the tin (pan), place on a wire rack and brush the top with the syrup glaze while still hot. Leave to cool before slicing.

BREAD & YEASTED DOUGH 103

CHOCOLATE

Chocolate Cheesecake with a Chocolate Puddle

Very rich, very indulgent, very chocolatey, totally sinful but oh so wonderful. This cheesecake is a real dinner party winner and a definite crowd pleaser, especially for the chocolate lovers in your life.

SERVES 8–10
Use a 21cm (8½ inch) round, 8cm (3¼ inch) deep loose-bottomed cake tin (pan)

BASE
20g (¾oz) hazelnuts, optional
45g (1½oz/3½ tbsp) unsalted butter
150g (5½oz) bourbon biscuits
15g (½oz/1 tbsp) caster (superfine) sugar
pinch of salt

FILLING
150g (5½oz) dark chocolate, broken into small pieces
600g (21oz) full-fat cream cheese at room temperature
100g (3½oz/½ cup) caster (superfine) sugar
30g (1¼oz/¼ cup) cornflour (cornstarch)
20g (¾oz/scant ¼ cup) cocoa powder, plus extra to decorate
½ tsp vanilla bean paste
300ml (10fl oz/1¼ cups) double (heavy) cream
2 eggs

CHOCOLATE PUDDLE
75g (2¾oz) milk chocolate
20g (¾oz/1½ tbsp) butter
1 tbsp golden syrup
80ml (3fl oz/⅓ cup) double (heavy) cream
chocolate shavings (optional)

Preheat the oven to 160°C fan/180°C/350°F/gas 4. Grease and line the tin (pan) with non-stick baking paper.

First, make the base. Toast the hazelnuts, if using, in a dry frying pan (skillet), tossing occasionally so they don't burn. Remove from the heat and leave to cool. Melt the butter in a small pan and set both to one side.

Separate the biscuits, remove the cream centre and discard. Place the biscuits, nuts, sugar and a pinch of salt in a food processor fitted with the blade attachment and blitz until everything resembles fine breadcrumbs. Add the melted butter, pulsing until it has been mixed through. Add the biscuit mix to the tin (pan) and press it down, covering the base in an even layer. Bake for 20 minutes, then leave to cool. Turn the oven down to 120°C fan/140°C/275°F/gas 1.

Now, make the filling. Place the chocolate in a heatproof bowl set over a pan of simmering water. Melt the chocolate, remove from the heat and set aside. Place the cream cheese, sugar, cornflour (cornstarch), cocoa, vanilla and cream in the bowl of a free-standing mixer and beat together using the paddle attachment. Add one egg at a time, continuing to beat until the mixture is smooth. Add the melted chocolate and give one final mix. Pour the thick chocolatey mixture on top of the pre-cooked biscuit base and bake for about 1½ hours or until just set. A slight wobble towards the centre should still be evident.

Switch off the oven, open the door slightly and leave the cheesecake inside to cool for an hour. This prevents the cheesecake from cracking (don't get disheartened if it does crack, the chocolate ganache will hide it anyway). Remove from the oven and leave to cool completely at room temperature before taking it out of the tin – run a palette knife around the edge to make this easier. Place in the fridge, loosely covered for at least 6 hours to firm up.

To make the chocolate puddle, gently melt the chocolate, butter and syrup together in a heatproof bowl set above a pan of simmering water. Stir until smooth and combined, then add half the cream, stirring to incorporate completely before adding the rest. Remove the cheesecake from the fridge and dust around the edges with cocoa. Pour the ganache into the centre of the cheesecake to create a chocolate puddle. Sprinkle on some chocolate shavings if you wish. The cheesecake will benefit from reaching room temperature before slicing and serving. Serve with pouring cream or crème fraîche.

Chocolate Mousse

A rich chocolate mousse is a simple yet luxurious dessert. Made in advance and set in pretty glasses, it will need little more attention other than being taken to the table. I adorn the top of each serving with Meringue Kisses, grated chocolate and softly whipped cream – the addition of some texture and decoration only adding to the luxury.

SERVES 6–8

100g (3½oz) dark chocolate, broken into small pieces
125g (4½oz) milk chocolate, broken into small pieces
20g (¾oz/1½ tbsp) unsalted butter
3 eggs, separated
½ tsp vanilla bean paste (optional)
150ml (5fl oz/scant ⅔ cup) double (heavy) cream

TOPPINGS (OPTIONAL)
Meringue Kisses (see page 26)
grated chocolate
softly whipped cream

Place the chocolate in a large heatproof bowl set above a pan of simmering water. Give the chocolate a stir every so often until completely melted and smooth, then remove from the heat. Add the butter, stirring until melted, then add the egg yolks one at a time, stirring between each addition. It may look like something has gone wrong at this point, the rich egg yolks fighting to combine with the chocolate. If it does, don't worry – simply add a splash of cream and whisk together until smooth, then set aside.

Add the vanilla, if using, to the cream and whisk to soft peaks either by hand or in a mixer. Be careful not to over work the cream; a nice silky dropping consistency is what is needed.

Whisk the egg whites either by hand or in a mixer until they are just holding shape. To test if they have been whisked enough, tip the bowl to one side, if they don't move, they are ready. Use a large metal spoon or spatula to carefully add one-third of both the whipped cream and the whisked egg whites into the chocolate and whisk in a brisk and rapid fashion. Incorporating the first third of each in this way should prevent the mousse from going grainy. Add the remainder of the cream and the egg whites and gentle fold both in together, trying to retain as much volume and air in the mousse as possible.

Spoon equally between the serving glasses and leave to set in the fridge for at least 4 hours. Remove from the fridge an hour before serving and decorate each serving with some of the additional toppings if desired.

Chocolate & Aubergine (Eggplant) Brownies

Chocolate and aubergine (eggplant) may seem like an odd combination but it works really well. I first came across this double act in Minori, an Italian seaside town on the Amalfi coast. This is my take on that combination, which is more like a brownie than the traditional dessert of the area, and no doubt would have many a Mamma from Campania questioning my changes! I urge you to give this a try as it will surprise you. Unlike a traditional brownie, it is light and moist due to the water content in the aubergines (eggplants). For those who like a good chocolate hit, it is extremely chocolatey... oh, and it's gluten free too.

MAKES 16 BROWNIES

Use a 21cm (8½ inch) square, 5cm (2 inch) deep baking tin (pan)

1kg (2¼lb) aubergines/ eggplants (about 3 medium-sized ones)

100g (3½oz) dark chocolate, broken into small pieces

100g (3½oz) milk chocolate, broken into small pieces

100g (3½oz/½ cup/1 stick) unsalted butter

100g (3½oz/½ cup) caster (superfine) sugar

4 eggs

pinch of salt

150g (5½oz/1½ cups) ground almonds (almond meal)

icing (powdered) sugar, to finsh (optional)

Preheat the oven to 180°C fan/200°C/400°F/gas 6. Grease and line the tin (pan) with non-stick baking paper.

Place the whole aubergines (eggplants) on a foil-lined baking sheet and bake for about 45–60 minutes, or until the flesh is tender and the skin has wrinkled. Carefully remove from the oven and leave until cool enough to handle. Slice down the length of each aubergine (eggplant) and scoop the pulpy flesh from each, discarding any tougher or seedy parts, and place in a sieve or colander sat above a bowl. As the flesh cools in the sieve, most of the excess liquid will drain into the bowl below. Leave to drain for 2 hours, then blitz in a food processer until pulpy.

Next, preheat the oven to 160°C fan/180°C/350°F/gas 4. Place the chocolate and butter in a heatproof bowl set over a pan of simmering water. Allow the butter and chocolate to melt, then stir until smooth and glossy. Remove from the heat, leave to cool, then add the drained aubergine (eggplant) flesh.

Place the sugar and eggs in the bowl of a free-standing mixer fitted with the whisk attachment. Whisk together on a high speed for 5 minutes until they become pale, fluffy and have increased considerably in volume. Add one-third of the whisked eggs, a pinch of salt and the almonds to the chocolate and aubergines (eggplants) and fold everything together. When combined, add the remaining whisked eggs, folding in gently – trying to keep as much air in place as possible. Pour the batter in to the tin, holding the mixing bowl close while doing so, to prevent any air from being lost in the process.

Bake in the centre of the oven for 45 minutes, after which turn the temperature down to 140°C fan/160°C/325°F/gas 3. Bake for a further 15 minutes, then check the brownie by inserting a skewer in to the centre; if it comes out relatively clean, it is ready (it does need to be a little fudgy). If the cake isn't quite ready, return it to the oven and bake for a further 10 minutes before re-checking.

Leave the brownies in the tin (pan) to cool a little before lifting out. Release the sides of the paper and leave to cool on a wire rack. When fully cooled, dust with icing (powdered) sugar, using a template for a patterned effect if you wish.

Triple Chocolate Celebration Cake

This cake has had many guises, the decoration techniques being the only alteration. This is my favourite way to present the cake, but you could use the icing and ganache to create many different finishes – perhaps leave the cake uncovered and pipe rounded domes of the icing between each layer instead. Whichever way you choose, the cake will be a hit and sure to please whoever is lucky enough to receive a slice.

SERVES 10–12

Use three 19cm (7½ inch) round, 3cm (1¼ inch) deep cake tins (pans)

350g (12oz/1½ cups/3 sticks) unsalted butter, softened

350g (12oz/1¾ cups) caster (superfine) sugar

6 eggs

350g (12oz/2⅔ cups) self-raising (self-rising) flour

1 tsp baking powder

60g (2oz/½ cup) cocoa powder

6 tbsp milk

CHOCOLATE FUDGE ICING

220g (8oz) chocolate – milk or dark or a mixture of both – broken into small pieces

150ml (5fl oz/scant ⅔ cup) double (heavy) cream

150g (5½oz/⅔ cup/1¼ sticks) unsalted butter

350g (12oz/3 cups) icing (powdered) sugar

CHOCOLATE GANACHE

150g (5½oz) milk chocolate, broken into small pieces

40g (1½oz/3 tbsp) butter

2 tbsp golden syrup

150ml (5fl oz/scant ⅔ cup) double (heavy) cream

DECORATIONS (OPTIONAL)

50g (1¾oz) milk or dark chocolate shavings, sprinkles

Preheat the oven to 160°C fan/180°C/350°F/gas 4. Grease and line the bottom of each tin (pan) with non-stick baking paper.

Place the butter and sugar in the bowl of a free-standing mixer fitted with the paddle attachment. Beat together for a few minutes until light in colour and fluffy in texture. Add 2 of the eggs, beat to combine and then add another 2, mixing well before adding the rest and scraping down the sides of the bowl if needs be. Sieve together the flour, baking powder and cocoa powder, then sieve once more onto the beaten mixture. Add the milk, then mix together briefly, stopping the moment that everything has come together and a smooth batter remains. Share the batter equally between each prepared tin (pan), weighing each if you wish. Smooth out the surface with the back of a spoon or palette knife.

Bake for 30 minutes, testing before removing from the oven. Insert a skewer into each cake; if the skewer comes out clean, they are ready. If needed, bake for a little longer then re-test. They may benefit from being turned or their positions swapped to ensure an even bake. When fully baked, remove from the oven and leave each in their tin (pan) for 2 minutes before turning out onto a wire rack. Remove the piece of baking paper and leave to cool completely.

To make the chocolate fudge icing, place the chocolate, cream and butter all together in a heatproof bowl set upon a pan of simmering water. When melted, remove from the heat and stir until smooth. Sieve in half of the icing (powdered) sugar, mixing and beating until smooth, then add the remainder and beat until thick. Set to one side, beating every so often to prevent a skin from forming.

To make the chocolate ganache, gently melt the chocolate, butter and syrup together in a heatproof bowl set above a pan of simmering water, stirring every so often. When melted and smooth, add one-third of the cream at a time, stirring to incorporate completely before adding the next. The ganache should be glossy and smooth. Leave to cool, stirring occasionally.

Prepare the cakes by slicing off any uneven tops, making each one flat and equal in size. Turn the first cake over and spread an even layer of the chocolate fudge icing over the surface, then place the second cake on top, turning the cake over to give a neater edge. Repeat with the fudge icing layer and top with the final cake. Use a palette knife to smooth some of the icing over the surface and around the sides of the cake, trying to keep the coating as even and smooth as possible.

Transfer the cake to a wire rack set above a large baking tray sheet or bowl. Give the ganache a quick stir, then pour a generous amount over the top of the cakes so it coats the surface and drips down the sides, covering the cake completely. Rescue any ganache that falls onto the baking sheet or bowl, return it to the remainder and pour over another layer. Leave to set a little while you prepare the decoration.

Spoon some of the icing and any remaining ganache into disposable piping (pastry) bags fitted with various nozzles (tips). Pipe out little mounds randomly across the surface of the cake in a decorative fashion. Highlight with some sprinkles, then use some shaved chocolate to decorate the sides and top of the cake.

Chocolate Fondants

The trick to getting chocolate fondants right is knowing your oven as they can differ so dramatically. I recommend using an oven thermometer for all of your cooking and baking, but especially when making these. It can be quite surprising how different the thermometer may read to that of which your dial is set. If you don't have a thermometer it would be a good idea to test bake one fondant before cooking the whole batch – you can then adjust the baking time if needs be. And remember, peering into the oven biting your nails really isn't necessary, they will work!

MAKES 8 FONDANTS
Use 8 small 180ml (6fl oz) non-stick pudding moulds

150g (5½oz) dark chocolate, broken into small pieces

200g (7oz) milk chocolate, broken into small pieces

50g (1¾oz/3½ tbsp) unsalted butter, softened

140g (5oz/scant ¾ cup) caster (superfine) sugar

4 eggs

1 tsp vanilla bean paste (optional)

60g (2oz/½ cup) plain (all-purpose) flour

Preheat the oven to 200°C fan/220°C/425°F/gas 7 and place a baking sheet inside. Grease the insides of each pudding mould and place a disc of non-stick baking paper in the bottom of each.

Melt the chocolate in a heatproof bowl sat upon a pan of simmering water. When melted, remove from the heat and start to make the batter.

Cream together the butter and sugar using a free-standing mixer fitted with a paddle attachment. Beat the eggs in a separate jug, adding the vanilla if using. Slowly add the eggs to the butter and sugar, continuing to mix as you do so, scraping down the sides of the bowl if needs be. Once all of the eggs are in, sieve over the flour and give a very brief mix, just until the flour has been combined. Add the melted chocolate, then stir together using a spatula until all of the chocolate has been evenly incorporated and the batter is smooth.

Pour or spoon the batter equally between the moulds, place each on the pre-heated baking tray sheet and cook for 11 minutes. Remove from the oven and leave the fondants in the moulds to rest for 1 minute.

To turn out, place an inverted plate on top of the mould and carefully turn over, lift off the mould and remove the piece of baking paper that will be on top of each fondant. Serve straight away with a generous glug of Vanilla Cream (see page 52) or ice cream if preferred.

Salted Caramel & Chocolate Tart

Soft and luxurious, this chocolate tart is a real treat and one I usually reserve for the adults. The layer of the salted caramel only adds to the luxury. It does, however, need a bit of forward planning as the chocolate layer needs plenty of time to set in the fridge prior to slicing.

SERVES 10–12

Use a 23cm (9 inch) round, 3cm (1¼ inch) deep tin (pan)

PASTRY

1 quantity of Sweet Shortcrust Pastry (see page 15), with 1 tsp vanilla bean paste added

SALTED CARAMEL

50g (1¾oz/¼ cup) caster (superfine) sugar

100ml (3½fl oz/generous ⅓ cup) water

150ml (5fl oz/scant ⅔ cup) double (heavy) cream

15g (½oz/1 tbsp) unsalted butter

½ tsp vanilla bean paste

pinch of sea salt, plus extra for sprinkling

CHOCOLATE LAYER

2 eggs

150ml (5fl oz/scant ⅔ cup) milk

200ml (7fl oz/generous ¾ cup) double (heavy) cream

150g (5½oz) dark chocolate, broken into small pieces

200g (7oz) milk chocolate, broken into small pieces

TO FINISH (OPTIONAL)

cocoa powder, for dusting

40g (1½oz) milk or dark chocolate

sprinkles

Make, line and blind bake your pastry as instructed on pages 13–15. Leave the pastry to cool completely, then trim off any excess, leaving the finished pastry case (shell) in the tin (pan).

Now, make the salted caramel layer. Rest a pastry brush in a cup of water. Pour the sugar into a heavy-based pan and add the water. Stir until the sugar has dissolved, then set over a medium heat. Run the dipped pastry brush around the inside of the pan, washing down any sugar crystals to prevent any unintended crystallization. Do this 2 more times during the cooking process. Bring to the boil and continue bubbling until the colour starts to change, swirling the pan from time to time to help the caramel cook and colour evenly. As the caramel edges closer to being ready, the bubbles will become bigger and the sounds from the pan will differ. Once the caramel has a golden amber hue, pour in half the cream, whisking briefly. Reduce the heat and leave to simmer for 2 minutes. Add the butter, vanilla, salt and remaining cream, giving all a good whisk until combined, then leave the sauce to simmer for a few minutes longer until thickened. Leave to cool and thicken a little, then pour into the cooked and cooled pastry case (shell). Dot the surface with a generous sprinkling of crushed salt flakes, then set aside to set further.

Now, make the chocolate layer. Add the eggs to a large bowl and lightly beat together. In a large pan, heat the milk and cream and bring to the boil, removing from the heat as it does. Pour a little of the hot cream onto the eggs, whisking continuously, then add the remainder. Add the chocolate to the hot liquid. Stir until all of the chocolate has melted and the mixture is smooth. Leave to cool for 30 minutes, then place in the fridge for an hour or so until it starts to thicken. Pour over the top of the caramel, filling the pastry case (shell) to the very top. Place back into the fridge and leave to set for at least 8 hours, ideally overnight.

Remove the tart from the fridge and place a doily over the top. Use some cocoa powder in a small sieve to dust a fine layer over the top. Lift off the doily to reveal a lacy cocoa pattern underneath. Use a vegetable peeler to grate some of the chocolate and use this to decorate around the outer edge of the tart, then add some sprinkles if you wish. Leave the tart to reach room temperature before serving. Slice into portions using a heated blade.

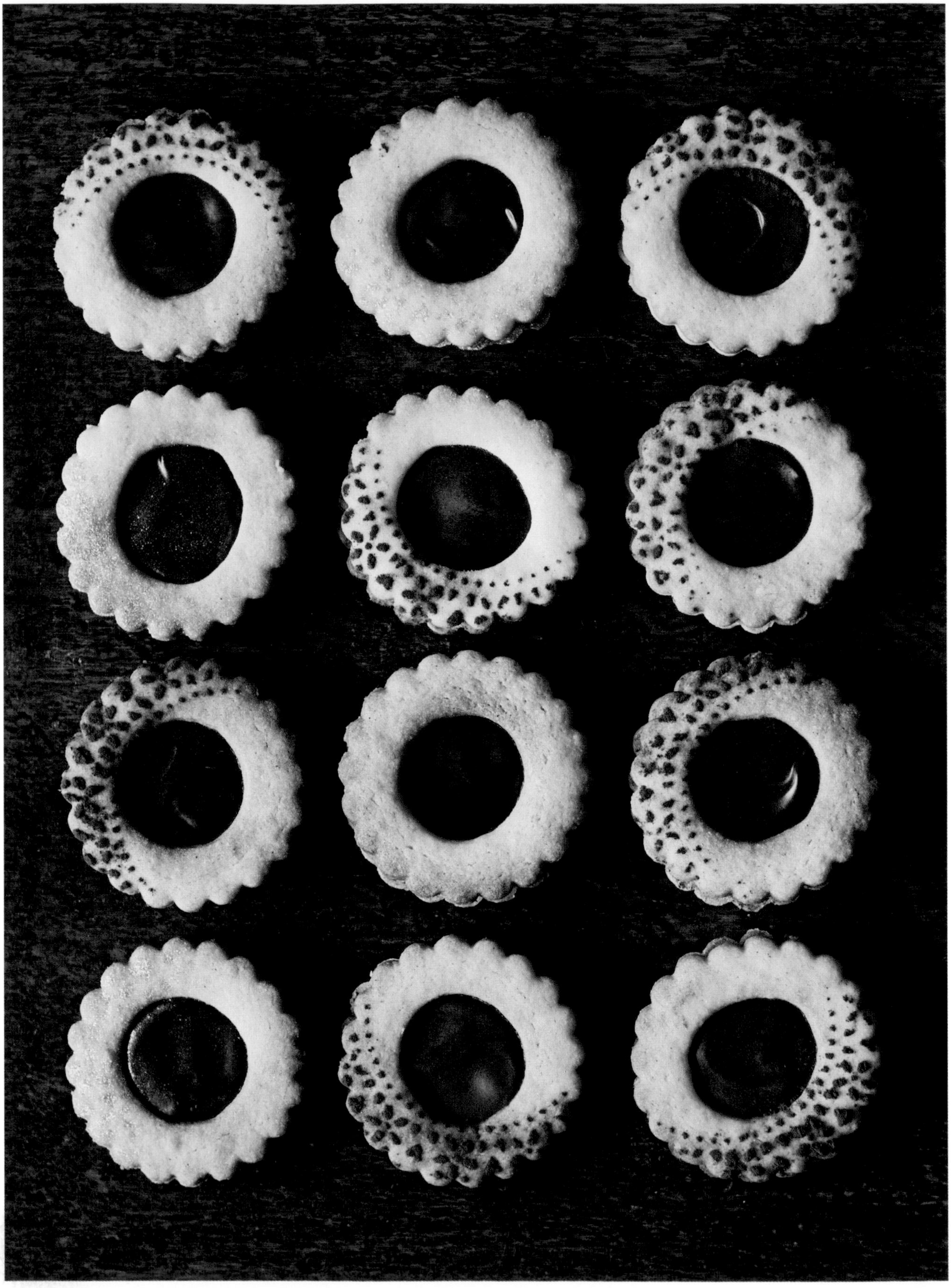

Chocolate Ganache Biscuits (Cookies)

I first made these biscuits (cookies) after thinking of ways to make a dent in the Easter chocolate hoard one year. With seemingly never-ending supplies of chocolate eggs and bars spilling out of the treats cupboard, it was too tempting for a baker to resist a bit of creative baking! These sandwich cookies are a real treat and if you use dark chocolate the kids just might leave you some! These would make a nice gift too.

MAKES 20–25 SANDWICH-BISCUITS (COOKIES)

90g (3oz/scant ½ cup/¾ stick) unsalted butter, softened
100g (3½oz/½ cup) caster (superfine) sugar
1 egg
½ tsp vanilla bean paste (optional)
200g (7oz/1½ cups) plain (all-purpose) flour, plus extra for dusting
¼ tsp baking powder
pinch of salt

FILLING & FINISHING

100g (3½oz) milk or dark chocolate, broken into pieces
20g (¾oz/1½ tbsp) unsalted butter
1 tbsp golden syrup
75ml (2¾fl oz/⅓ cup) double (heavy) cream
cocoa powder, for dusting

Place the butter and sugar in the bowl of a free-standing mixer fitted with the paddle attachment. Beat for 2 minutes until both are light and fluffy. Add the egg and vanilla and continue beating until combined, scraping down the sides of the bowl if needs be. Sieve the dry ingredients together, then re-sieve into the mixing bowl. Beat once more until a cohesive dough has formed but do stop mixing the moment that everything comes together. Turn out onto a large piece of clingfilm (plastic wrap) and bring the dough together to form a ball. Flatten out with the palms of your hands, then wrap tightly in the clingfilm (plastic wrap) and place in the fridge for at least 1 hour to chill and firm up a bit.

Preheat the oven to 180°C fan/200°C/400°F/gas 6. Line 2 baking sheets with non-stick baking paper.

Remove the dough from the fridge and place on a floured surface, dusting the surface of the dough too. Roll out to 3mm (⅛ inch) thick, moving it around as you do so to make sure it doesn't stick, and adding more flour if needed. Cut out 40-50 biscuit (cookie) shapes (you'll need two per biscuit/cookie), using a 6cm (2½ inch) round fluted cutter, then use a 3cm (1¼ inch) round cutter to cut the centre from half the rounds. Transfer the cookies to the baking sheets, leaving a space between each – you may need to bake in batches.

Bake for 10–12 minutes, or until golden. When cooked, remove from the oven, leaving to cool for a minute before transferring them to a wire rack.

Have a disposable piping (pastry) bag to hand. Melt 25g (1oz) of the chocolate in the microwave for 30–60 seconds. Once completely melted, pour into the piping (pastry) bag, leave to cool for a few minutes, then snip off the end.
Lay the whole cookies out in rows, turning each one over. Use the melted chocolate to pipe a border around the outside edge of each biscuit, then leave to set (this will stop the ganache from sliding off when filling).

To make the ganache, place the remaining chocolate in a heatproof bowl sat above a pan of simmering water. Add the butter and syrup and allow everything to melt. When melted, glossy and smooth, remove from the heat and add the cream a little at first, stirring between each addition, then leave to cool.

Spoon a generous dollop of ganache onto each cookie base, spreading it out to meet the chocolate border. Top each with the remaining cookies, then dust some cocoa powder through a doily or template to create a decorative pattern. Leave to set fully before eating.

DESSERTS

Crystallized Flowers

Decorating cakes and desserts with crystallized flowers is a guaranteed way to make everything that little bit prettier. They are easy to do and can be used to adorn cakes, give a burst of colour to a pavlova or could even be served alongside a panna cotta. All you need is a light touch, a soft-tipped brush and a water sprayer.

MAKES 30–40 FLOWERS
*depending on the size of the
   flower or petal used*

edible flowers such as violas,
   roses, violets, polyanthus,
   borage or sweet Williams
1 egg white
caster (superfine) sugar, for
   sprinkling

To clean the flowers, spray each with a very fine mist of water, then place on to some kitchen paper to dry.

Remove the flower head from the stem, leaving the part that holds the flower together in place. Working with 1 flower at a time, lay onto the flattened fingertips of an out-stretched hand, underside facing up.

Use a small round-tipped brush to gently coat each petal with a light layer of egg white, lifting any overlapping petals if needs be. Spoon some sugar into a fine sieve and shake over the flower, giving it a fine dusting. Gently turn the flower over and repeat. Continue until all of the flowers have been used.

Lay the crystallized flowers on some non-stick baking paper and leave to dry for at least 24 hours.

Vanilla Baked Cheesecake with Seasonal Fruits

I find baked cheesecakes to be far more indulgent than their gelatine set cousins. They are rich, creamy and incredibly smooth and make for a very luxurious dessert indeed. Baking the cheesecake at a lower temperature for a longer time should hold off any unsightly cracks and will also prevent any colour from being taken. One important piece of advice that I will pass to you (learned through experience) is to ensure that the tin (pan) you use is leak-proof. There is no fun in seeing all of your careful preparation leaking out of the tin (pan), covering the bottom of your oven!

SERVES 8–10

Use a 21cm (8½ inch) round, 6cm (2½ inch) deep loose-bottomed cake tin (pan)

BASE

90g (3oz/scant ½ cup/¾ stick)unsalted butter
200g (7oz) crunchy oat cookies
pinch of salt

FILLING

500g (1lb 2oz) full-fat cream cheese at room temperature
100g (3½oz/½ cup/1 stick) unsalted butter at room temperature
80ml (3fl oz/⅓ cup) double (heavy) cream
200g (7oz/1 cup) caster (superfine) sugar
2 tsp vanilla bean paste
30g (1¼oz/¼ cup) cornflour (cornstarch)
5 eggs

FRUIT

400g (14oz) mixed summer berries or seasonal alternatives
2 tbsp icing (powdered) sugar
100ml (3½fl oz/generous ⅓ cup) water
juice of 1 lemon

Preheat the oven to 160°C fan/180°C/350°F/gas 4. Line the base and sides of the tin (pan) with non-stick baking paper.

First, make the base. Gently melt the butter in a small pan and set aside. Crush the cookies to a fine crumb, either by hand or in a food processor and add a pinch of salt. Pour in the melted butter and combine well. Press the mixture evenly into the base of the lined tin (pan), smoothing out evenly with the back of a spoon. Bake for 15 minutes, then remove and leave to cool completely.

Turn the oven down to 100°C fan/120°C/240°F/gas ¼–½.

Beat together the cream cheese and the butter until smooth – it is important that both are at room temperature to ensure that the mix will be lump free. When smooth and well combined, add the cream, sugar, vanilla and cornflour (cornstarch). Mix until smooth, then beat in the eggs. Pour over the base, removing any air bubbles that rise to the surface.

Bake in the cooler oven for up to 2 hours, checking after the first hour, then again 30 minutes later. The cheesecake should have a slight wobble towards the centre when ready. Only remove from the oven at this point if you feel that it has set sufficiently, otherwise continue to cook for longer. That said, it is worth bearing in mind that the cheesecake will continue to set as it is cools. Remove from the oven but do leave it in the tin (pan) until completely cooled. Refrain from putting the cheesecake in the fridge as it will change the consistency completely, losing its luxury.

Wash and prepare the fruit, halving any larger berries. Add to a pan along with the sugar and water and gently simmer for 3 minutes. Transfer to a bowl and add a few drops of lemon juice – a certain level of tartness is a welcome contrast to the richness of the cheesecake.

Slice and serve with some of the fruit spooned over the top.

Vanilla Panna Cotta with Caramel Shards & Seasonal Fruits

I'll never forget the first panna cotta I ever tasted – it was so disappointing! With a texture not dissimilar to rubber, it was nothing like I had imagined. My opinions were only swayed some years later, giving the dessert another try while out for lunch. Making its way to the table with a mesmerizing wobble, I knew this was going to be a completely different experience. It was soft and creamy and it melted the moment it hit my mouth. Panna cotta has been, and will remain, one of my favourite desserts ever since.

SERVES 6–8

4 sheets of premium-grade leaf gelatine
800ml (28fl oz/3⅓ cups) double (heavy) cream
150ml (5fl oz/scant ⅔ cup) milk
200g (7oz/1 cup) caster (superfine) sugar
1 tsp vanilla bean paste
selection of seasonal fruits, to serve

CARAMEL SHARDS

200g (7oz/1 cup) caster (superfine) sugar
100ml (3½fl oz/generous ⅓ cup) water

Set out the moulds, glasses or ramekins in which the panna cotta will be set.

Place the gelatine sheets in a bowl and cover with cold water. Pour the cream and the milk into a pan and add the sugar and vanilla. Set over a medium heat and bring to the boil, removing from the heat as soon as it does so.

Lift the gelatine from the bowl, patting it onto a clean tea towel to remove any excess water, then add it to the hot cream. Whisk until the gelatine has completely dissolved, then pass the cream through a sieve into a large jug or bowl.

The moulds could be filled at this point but the vanilla seeds will sink to the bottom – if, like me, you like to see the vanilla seeds equally distributed throughout, leave the mixture to thicken considerably before doing so. Share the thickened panna cotta between each mould or glass and leave to set in the fridge for at least 8 hours.

When making the caramel shards, line a heatproof surface with non-stick baking paper and have a pastry brush and a cup of water to hand. Place the sugar in a heavy-based pan and add the water. Stir to dissolve the sugar, then place over a medium heat. Run a wet pastry brush around the sides of the pan, washing down any sugar crystals, preventing any unintended crystallization. Heat the sugar until the sugar solution changes to a golden amber. Pour the hot caramel onto the baking paper, lifting and tilting the paper so that the caramel runs downwards. As the caramel starts to set, move the paper around to create a thin layer. Leave the caramel to set, then break it into shards. Store between sheets of non-stick baking paper in an airtight container until needed.

When the panna cotta has set, turn them out of the moulds by dipping each vessel into a bowl filled with hot water. Place a plate on top of the mould then invert, giving one firm shake. The panna cotta should come out easily.

Prepare the fruits, by washing, slicing, chopping and dicing; the different cuts adding to the final presentation. Arrange a selection of fruit on and around the panna cotta; rest a caramel shard or two against the sides, and one on top.

White Chocolate Crème Brûlée Tart

This dessert really does have the wow factor. Softly cooked, creamy custard encased in a crisp pastry case (shell) with the added caramel crunch of the bruléed top. Crème brûlée is my absolute favourite dessert, and serving it in a tart and enriching it further with white chocolate only adds to its splendour. I love the way you can slice the tart at the table – the satisfying crunch when the top cracks will never fail to make any awaiting guest all the more eager. The custard can be cooked in the traditional manner if you prefer, just pour into individual ramekins, set in a bain-marie and bake in the oven until set, then brûlée each before serving.

SERVES 10–12
*Use a 23cm (9 inch) round,
3.5cm (1½ inch) deep tart
tin (pan)*

PASTRY
1 quantity of Sweet
   Shortcrust Pastry
   (see page 15)

FILLING
8 egg yolks
1 tbsp caster (superfine) sugar
600ml (1 pint/2½ cups)
   double (heavy) cream
1 tsp vanilla bean paste
300g (10½oz) white
   chocolate, broken into
   small pieces

FRUIT
300g (10½oz) soft seasonal
   berries, washed
2 tsp caster (superfine) sugar
juice of ½ a lemon

FINISHING
3 tbsp caster (superfine) sugar
blow torch
white chocolate, for shaving

Make, line and blind bake the pastry as instructed on pages 13–15. Leave the pastry to cool completely, then trim off the excess, leaving the cooked case (shell) in its tin (pan) while you make the white chocolate custard. Preheat the oven to 110°C fan/130°C/250°F/gas ½.

Place the egg yolks in a large bowl along with the sugar and whisk together until combined. Put the cream and vanilla in a pan and bring to the boil, removing from the heat as soon as it does so. Pour a little of the hot cream onto the egg yolks and give them a whisk through. Add a little more of the cream and then pour in the rest, whisking well. Add the chocolate pieces to the hot cream and stir until the chocolate has melted and the mixture is smooth.

Place the blind baked pastry case (shell), still in its tin (pan), on a baking sheet. Open the oven door and pull out the middle shelf a little. Place the baking sheet and pastry case (shell) on the shelf and pour the white chocolate custard into the pastry case (shell), filling as deeply as you can – there will be some custard left over, this could be baked in separate ramekins in a bain-marie if you so wish. Gently ease the shelf back into the oven, close the door and cook for about 1 hour, checking the tart after about 45 minutes. When ready, the custard should only have a slight wobble towards the centre when given a gentle shake. If you feel it is still too wobbly towards the outer parts of the tart, bake it for a further 15 minutes and then re-check, repeating the process until you have just the right amount of wobble! The tart can go from being seemingly under cooked to being solidly set in minutes, so be vigilant! It will keep setting as it cools too. Once you are happy with the wobble, remove from the oven and leave to cool completely.

Meanwhile, prepare the fruit. Place the berries in a bowl and sprinkle with the sugar. Squeeze in a generous amount of lemon juice and leave to macerate for 30 minutes.

Sprinkle the surface of the tart evenly with 2 tablespoons of the sugar. Set the flame on your blow torch to maximum and heat the sugar until it melts and starts to caramelize. Move the flame swiftly, trying not to hold it in one place for too long as it will have an effect on the cooked custard below. Sprinkle over the remaining sugar (if needed) and repeat until you have a satisfyingly bruléed top. To serve, slice the tart into portions and serve with some of the macerated fruit and add some shaved white chocolate to decorate.

Iles Flôttantes

I once served this dessert to the legendary chef Pierre Koffmann, under the guidance and mentorship of Bryn Williams. Upon serving Pierre this French classic he declared that we had made him his favourite dessert – no pressure then. With bated breath, we waited for the verdict. 'Perfect!' was his response. It was quite something to receive such praise from a culinary legend! It is easy to see why this dessert is a favourite to many – from children to culinary greats alike, it never fails to comfort and please. I have made this dessert many times since, each time serving it with a recital of the story.

SERVES 6

1 lemon wedge
100g (3½oz) egg whites
100g (3½oz/½ cup) caster (superfine) sugar
400ml (14fl oz/ 1½ cups) milk for Crème Anglaise (see page 137)

CARAMEL
100g (3½oz/½ cup) caster (superfine) sugar
50ml (2fl oz/scant ¼ cup) water

Rub the inside of a mixing bowl with a wedge of lemon and add the weighed egg whites. Whisk on a medium speed until soft peaks form, tipping the bowl to one side to see if they are ready – if the egg whites slide, whisk for a minute longer. Turn the mixer up a notch and start to add the sugar 1 spoonful at a time, allowing each spoonful to be whisked through before adding the next. When all of the sugar has been added and the meringues are thick and smooth, rub a little of the meringue between your fingers. If you can feel grains of sugar, whisk for a minute more then test again. When smooth, set aside.

Pour the milk into a large frying pan (skillet) set above a low heat, warming the milk until it reaches a gentle simmer. Dip a large metal spoon into some hot water, then scoop out 6 generous portions of meringue, placing each onto the simmering milk. Poach the meringues for 10 minutes, turning them over halfway through and maintaining that gentle simmer throughout. Use a slotted spoon to remove each from the milk and set on a clean tea towel.

Pass the poaching milk through a sieve into a measuring jug – 300ml (10fl oz/ 1¼ cups) of the milk is needed for the Crème Anglaise so do top up with fresh milk if needs be.

Make the Crème Anglaise as instructed on page 137. Once the custard has cooled, pour it into a serving bowl and top with the poached meringues.

Make a caramel as instructed on page 131. Carefully drizzle the hot caramel over the poached meringues and serve.

Crème Anglaise

Some things just need lashings of custard, without it they just aren't quite the same, take apple pie or stewed rhubarb for an example. My Nana used to make custard at least once a week, served over a variety of desserts, every one simple but suddenly all the more luxurious because of it. It's just so comforting, whenever I taste custard it instantly reminds me of great home-cooked comfort food. It really is worth making your own, especially if you make the Deep-filled Apple Pie on page 32, but it can be poured over anything from a sliced banana to sticky sponge pudding and makes everything all the better for it.

SERVES 6–8

300ml (10fl oz/1¼ cups) milk
300ml (10fl oz/1¼ cups) double (heavy) cream
1 tsp vanilla bean paste
100g (3½oz/½ cup) caster (superfine) sugar
8 egg yolks

Place the milk, cream, vanilla and 60g (2oz/⅔ cup) of the sugar in a heavy-based pan and gently bring to the boil, removing from the heat the moment that it does so. Set to one side and leave the vanilla flavour to infuse into the hot milk while you prepare the egg yolks.

Place the egg yolks in a large bowl (keeping the whites for another use). Sprinkle the remaining sugar onto the egg yolks and whisk together for a minute or so until they are thickened and have turned pale (this will help to thicken the custard during cooking). Add a little of the vanilla milk to the yolks and whisk to combine, then add the rest, giving everything a final whisk through. Pour the mixture back into the pan and set over a low heat. Start to gently heat, stirring continually. You only need to cook the custard for about 3–4 minutes, enough for it to thicken slightly. If cooked for too long or at too high a temperature, the egg yolks will over cook and scramble giving you a lumpy sauce. Remove from the heat as soon as the sauce coats the back of a spoon and pour it through a sieve into a serving jug or bowl.

Serve hot or cold.

Bread & Butter Pudding

Bread and butter pudding seems to have come back in to favour over recent years, the modern versions holding more elaborate and expensive ingredients inside. It's such a simple dessert, but one that holds very fond memories for me. I prefer the more traditional pudding with nutmeg and dried fruits being the only additions – simple is often best. Use some leftover homemade bread if you have it – both the Braided Challah (see page 96) and the Caramel Bread (see page 98) work well. If using the Caramel Bread, you could enhance the caramel flavour by stirring a tablespoon of caramel sauce into some hot milk before using it to make up the custard.

SERVES 4–6

Use a 20 x 25cm (8 x 10 inch) baking dish

100g (3½oz/½ cup/1 stick) unsalted butter, softened

2 tbsp demerara sugar

60g (2oz) mixed dried fruits – golden raisins, sultanas, currants

12 slices of sliced white bread (or leftover homemade bread if available), more slices may be required depending on loaf size

4 eggs

350ml (12fl oz/1½ cups) milk

200ml (7fl oz/generous ¾ cup) double (heavy) cream

80g (2¾oz/⅓ cup) caster (superfine) sugar

½ a nutmeg

Preheat the oven to 160°C fan/180°C/350°F/gas 4. Lightly grease the baking dish with some of the butter, then sprinkle over a little of the demerara sugar and scatter in some of the dried fruit.

Cut shapes from the bread slices if you wish, then spread each piece generously with the remaining butter. Lay the bread over the base of the dish, then scatter over the rest of the fruit. Repeat with the remaining bread, arranging the pieces so that they overlap each other in a decorative manner.

Beat the eggs in a bowl or jug and add the milk, cream and caster (superfine) sugar. Whisk to combine, then pour into the dish and leave to stand for 15 minutes while the bread soaks up some of the custard. Tuck any fruit that has surfaced underneath the bread slices as they can burn easily. Sprinkle the surface with the remaining demerara sugar and finish with a generous grating of nutmeg.

Bake for 35–40 minutes until just set and golden. The pudding will puff up beautifully so hot foot it over to the dining table so everyone can see it before it sinks. Leave to cool a little before serving it with some cream. This is comfort pudding at is best.

Charlotte Royale

I'm often looking for new things to make, taking one idea from one thing, playing with it and making something new. While searching for some inspiration one afternoon, I stumbled across this retro-looking dessert and I just had to give it a go. I'd never seen anything like it before, so off I set recreating my own. It does require a bit of effort but like most things in this book, it can be broken down into stages. Whenever I have made this (usually for a special occasion), my guests have always been wowed and intrigued by it as it's not a dessert you see every day.

SERVES 10–12

Use a 38 x 25cm (15 x 10 inch) Swiss roll tin (jelly roll pan) and a 2-litre (68-fl oz/8½-cup) rounded mixing bowl

SWISS ROLLS
A little butter for greasing
6 eggs
140g (5oz/¾ cup) caster (superfine) sugar, plus extra for sprinkling
150g (5½oz/generous 1 cup) plain (all-purpose) flour
½ tsp baking powder
200g (7oz) strawberry jam

STRAWBERRY BAVAROIS
6 x 13g (½oz) gelatine leaves
300ml (10fl oz/1¼ cups) milk
1 tsp vanilla bean paste
140g (5oz/¾ cup) caster (superfine) sugar
5 egg yolks
100g (3½oz) strawberries, quartered, plus extra to decorate
400ml (14fl oz/1⅔ cups) double (heavy) cream, plus extra for piping
300g (10½oz) strawberries, juiced or puréed, no pips

GLAZING & FINISHING
75g (2¾oz/⅓ cup) caster (superfine) sugar
1 tbsp arrowroot

Preheat the oven to 160°C fan/180°C/350°F/gas 4. Grease and line the Swiss roll tin (jelly roll pan) with non-stick baking paper and line the mixing bowl with clingfilm (plastic wrap).

First, make the Swiss rolls. Place the eggs and sugar in the bowl of a free-standing mixer and whisk until they look pale in colour and have increased considerably in volume – this will take at least 5 minutes. Sift the flour and baking powder together, then re-sift over the top of the whisked eggs. Gently fold the flour into the whisked eggs, taking great care as you do so, retaining as much of the air as possible.

Pour half of the mixture into the centre of the prepared tin (pan), holding the bowl close as you do so. Tilt the tin (pan) so the mixture runs into all 4 corners. When level (it will look quite flat), pop into the oven and bake for 10–12 minutes, until golden. A good way to check if the sponge is ready is to see if the baking paper peels away from the sides with ease.

While the sponge is baking, gently warm the jam (jelly) in a pan and set aside. Lay a clean tea towel horizontally on a work surface and spray it all over with water. Lay a piece of non-stick baking paper on top and sprinkle with caster (superfine) sugar.

When the sponge is ready, remove from the tray and invert onto the sugared paper, gently peeling back the baking paper. Score along the longest side of the sponge, starting 2cm (¾ inch) from the edge, and being careful not to cut all the way through. Brush the surface with half the jam (jelly) and use the scored edge as a starting point to roll up the sponge, using the sugared paper and the damp tea towel to help you.

When fully rolled, leave it wrapped in the paper and repeat the whole process making the second Swiss roll with the leftover mixture. When both Swiss rolls are cool, remove the paper and slice each into 1cm (½ inch) slices, eating or discarding the end pieces. Cover with clingfilm (plastic wrap) until needed.

continued overleaf

Now, make the bavarois. Place the gelatine in a container of cold water and leave to soften. Heat the milk, vanilla and 100g (3½oz/½ cup) of the sugar until boiling, then remove from the heat. Whisk together the egg yolks and the remaining sugar in a large bowl, then pour in a little of the hot milk, whisking to combine. Add the rest of the milk gradually, whisking as you do so, then return all to the pan and cook until thick enough to coat the back of a spoon.

Squeeze the water from the gelatine, draining any excess on a tea towel. Add to the hot custard, stirring until it has fully dissolved, then pour through a sieve into a large clean bowl and leave to cool, stirring every so often. When cooled, but not yet set, add the strawberry juice (or purée) and stir through. Whisk the cream into soft peaks, folding it into the bavarois, then set to one side.

Cover the inside of the lined bowl with slices of Swiss roll, placing each slice as close to the next as possible. Any visible gaps can be filled with some small pieces of Swiss roll if you wish. Reserve all remaining slices as these will form the bottom of the dessert.

Check the consistency of the bavarois, if it is still quite fluid, pop it in the fridge to thicken up a bit but do check every 10 minutes or so. When it is really thick, stir through the quartered strawberries and pour into the bowl lined with the Swiss roll slices. Top with the remaining Swiss roll, covering the surface of the bavarois completely. Cover with clingfilm (plastic wrap) and place in the fridge to set for at least 4 hours.

To turn the pudding out of the bowl, invert onto a large serving plate and remove the clingfilm (plastic wrap).

To glaze, tip the sugar into a small pan, add 100ml (3½fl oz/generous ⅓ cup) of water and bring to the boil. Dissolve the arrowroot in 2 tablespoons water and pour it into the sugar syrup. Bring back to the boil, then remove from the heat. Leave the mixture to cool a little before brushing it all over the Royale.

Whip a little more cream and pipe decoratively around the base, finishing with fresh strawberries and/or some redcurrants and fresh flowers.

Delizie al Limone

I was married in Minori, a small Italian seaside town along the Amalfi Coast. We wanted our reception to be in-keeping with the Italian tradition, which of course meant lots of delicious food. Course after course flowed out of that tiny kitchen of Villa Maria, all absolutely delicious, all plentiful and filling. Soon we were all visibly exasperated at the thought of having to eat anything else. When this epic meal finally came to an end, it was then declared that the dessert was ready and waiting! With a few gulps heard and the odd belt loosened, we all gathered around a table that held this traditional wedding cake. I'm sure we were all thinking the same – the thought of eating more food was quite impossible. However, we all duly accepted our portion and delved in. It was the lightest, most amazing cake that I have ever tasted, it was just wonderful and we all finished it with ease, some even going in for seconds! I have added a layer of my homemade Lemon Curd in my version.

SERVES 6
30 x 21cm (12 x 8 inch) baking sheet x 2

SPONGE LAYERS
butter, for greasing
5 eggs
170g (6oz/generous ¾ cup) caster (superfine) sugar
170g (6oz/scant 1¼ cups) plain (all-purpose) flour
1 tsp baking powder
3 tbsp Lemon Curd (see page 155, or shop bought)

LEMON CUSTARD
grated zest of 1½ lemons
500ml (18fl oz/2 cups) milk
80g (2¾oz/⅓ cup) caster (superfine) sugar
4 egg yolks
25g (1oz/3 tbsp) plain (all-purpose) flour
120ml (4fl oz/½ cup) double (heavy) cream

LIMONCELLO SYRUP
50g (1¾oz/¼ cup) caster (superfine) sugar
50ml (2fl oz/¼ cup) water
50ml (2fl oz/scant ¼ cup) limoncello

Preheat the oven to 160°C fan/180°C/350°F/gas 4. Grease and line the baking sheets.

First, make the sponge layers. Place the eggs and sugar in the bowl of a free-standing mixer and whisk for 5 minutes, or until they are pale in colour and have increased in volume considerably. Sieve the flour and baking powder together, then re-sift onto the whisked eggs. Gently fold in the flour until fully incorporated, doing so with care to retain as much of the air as possible.

Holding the bowl close to the baking sheets, share the batter equally between the tins, pouring into the centre of ech one. Tilt and lift the baking sheets to level the mixture, letting it run into all 4 corners. Bake for 10–12 minutes or until golden and springy to the touch. A good way to check if the sponge is ready, by pulling the paper away from the sides; if it comes away with ease it is ready. Once cooked, turn the sponges out of the baking sheets onto wire racks and gently remove the paper.

Next make the custard. Place the lemon zest, milk and 20g (¾oz/1 ¼ tablespoons) of the sugar in a pan, bring to the boil, then remove from the heat. Whisk the egg yolks with the remaining sugar, then whisk in the flour. Gradually add the hot milk to the egg mixture, combining well. Return all to the pan and leave the custard to bubble for 2 minutes, whisking continuously. Once the custard is thick and the taste of raw flour has gone, transfer to a bowl, cover the surface with clingfilm (plastic wrap), to stop a skin forming, and leave to cool before refrigerating until cold.

Now, make the syrup. Place the sugar and water in a small pan and gently heat until the sugar has dissolved. Increase the heat, letting it boil for a few minutes until a syrupy consistency is achieved. Leave to cool, then stir in the limoncello and set aside.

continued overleaf

Give the cooled lemon custard a vigorous whisk, until smooth and spoonable. Whip the cream until soft peaks form, then gently fold this into the custard.

Cut twelve 7cm (2¾ inch) rounds and six 5cm (2 inch) rounds out of the cooked sponges. Brush each sponge disc with the limoncello syrup and spread a layer of Lemon Curd over 6 of the larger discs, topping each with another large disc. To finish, spread a little Lemon Custard over the top of the large discs, then place a small disc on top.

Place each cake tower onto a wire rack set over a large clean baking sheet and spoon over enough of the lemon custard to completely cover – the excess will drip through the wire rack, which can be collected and reused. A second bathing may be needed to get a neat finish. Transfer the cakes to a large serving plate, arranging them close together. Any gaps can be filled by piping the remaining custard in to them. If the custard is a little too runny to hold a piped shape, thicken it with some stiffly whipped cream.

Decorate with some shavings of lemon zest, flowers and greenery and serve the plate in the middle of the table so your guests can help themselves. This dessert needs no further accompaniment, but you can never going wrong by adding a little glass of limoncello.

Meringue-Nest Sharing Wreath

This is just a decorative take on the classic combination of meringues, fruit and cream – a cross between a pavlova and a meringue nest. The wreath makes a great centrepiece to any dinner table and the toppings can be changed to suit the occasion.

SERVES 8

MERINGUES
1 lemon wedge
100g (3½oz) egg whites
200g (7oz/1 cup) caster (superfine) sugar

TOPPINGS
selection of seasonal fruits
Lemon Curd (see page 155 or shop bought, optional
1 quantity of Vanilla Cream (see page 52)

Preheat the oven to 100°C fan/120°C/240°F/gas ¼–½.

Use some non-stick baking paper to make the template for the wreath by drawing around a plate or something circular that measures about 22cm (8¾ inches) in diameter. Select a cup or glass that has a diameter of about 6cm (2½ inches), then draw around that, positioning it centrally over the outer line. Repeat until you have 8 small circles running around the larger circle, spacing each roughly 1cm (½ inch) apart. Turn the paper over so that the ink is underneath, preventing it from marking the base of your meringue. Use the paper to line a baking sheet.

To make the meringue, rub the inside of the mixing bowl with a wedge of lemon. Add the egg whites and whisk on a medium speed until they have formed soft peaks. To test if they are ready, tip the bowl slightly, if the egg whites stay put they are ready; if they slide, whisk for a minute longer. Turn the mixer to a high speed and start to add the sugar 1 dessertspoon at a time, allowing each to be whisked through before adding the next. When all of the sugar has been used and the meringue is stiff, rub a little between your fingers. If you can feel grains of sugar, continue to whisk for a minute or so until smooth. Transfer to a disposable piping (pastry) bag fitted with a star nozzle (tip).

Secure the paper template to the baking sheet using a little of the meringue underneath each corner. Pipe the individual circles first, starting in the centre of each and use a continuous flow, spiralling around until the outer line is reached. On top of the piped discs create a border around the outer edge of each, refilling the bag when necessary. The gaps between each meringue nest will also need to be filled, securing everything together as a wreath. Pipe more of the meringue decoratively in between each nest to do so.

Bake for 2 hours, or until completely crisp and cooked through. Check the underneath by gently lifting off the paper. If the meringue is still gooey or slightly wet, return to the oven until dry. Turn off the oven, leaving the wreath inside until the oven has completely cooled.

Prepare the fruits by washing, slicing, dicing and cutting, using different cuts to create a decorative finish, then set aside.

To assemble the wreath, place the meringue on a suitable plate or platter. If using the Lemon Curd, spoon a little into each nest. Top with the Vanilla Cream, serving any leftover at the table. Place the fruit and a few flower sprigs decoratively around the wreath, then serve.

Autumn Crumble

Fruit crumbles make a regular appearance in our house during the colder months, bringing comfort as the nights draw in. Apple and blackberry is a family favourite, made all the better when wild berries are used – picked from nearby hedgerows. The fruits used may change throughout these colder months, both pears and plums making a good alternative, and as winter gives way to spring, there is always the rhubarb season to look forward to. Pre-cooking the crumble topping isn't the traditional method but it does help to prevent any sogginess, and for that reason I much prefer doing it this way.

SERVES 4–6

Preheat the oven to 180°C fan/200°C/400°F/gas 6.

CRUMBLE TOPPING

50g (1¾oz/⅓ cup) plain (all-purpose) flour

50g (1¾oz/⅓ cup) wholemeal flour

25g (1oz/1½ tbsp) demerara sugar

50g (1¾ oz/¼ cup) caster (superfine) sugar

½ tsp ground ginger (optional)

100g (3½oz/½ cup/1 stick) unsalted butter

25g (1oz/4tbsp) rolled oats

FRUIT FILLING

750g (1lb 10oz) apples

50g (1¾oz/3½ tbsp) unsalted butter

50g (1¾oz/¼ cup) soft light brown sugar

½ tsp ground cinnamon (optional)

150g (5½oz) blackberries

2 figs (optional)

2 plums (optional)

DECORATIVE FINISH (OPTIONAL)

1 apple

1 plum

blackberries

To make the crumble topping, tip the flours, sugars and ginger, if using, into a large bowl and mix together. Dice the butter and add to the dry ingredients, rubbing it into the flour with a delicate touch. Add the oats and give everything a mix together. Lay the crumble mixture out on a baking sheet and bake for 15–20 minutes, giving the crumble a mix halfway through. Transfer to a plate and set aside.

Prepare the apples by peeling, coring and cutting them into 3cm (1¼ inch) chunks and place them in a medium pan. Add 30g (1¼oz) of the butter, the sugar and cinnamon, if using, along with 50ml (2fl oz/scant ¼ cup) of water. Set over a low heat and gently simmer for 10 minutes or until the apples soften.

In the meantime, wash and prepare the other fruit (if using). Remove the woody stalk from the figs and the stones from the plums, then cut each in to 8 pieces, adding them to the pan along with the whole blackberries. Cook for a further 2 minutes.

Use a slotted spoon to transfer the fruit to a suitable baking dish, leaving behind the juices. Add the remaining butter to the pan and turn the heat up a little, allowing the butter to melt. Simmer for 2–3 minutes, until the juices have reduced and thickened, then add to the fruit and stir everything together. Top generously with the blind baked crumble and bake for 20 minutes, or until the crumble is golden and crisp and pockets of sticky fruit juice start to bubble at the edges. Serve with a generous glug of homemade custard – comfort bathed in comfort.

Variation: If you wanted to serve the crumble with the addition of the decorative fruit as in the image opposite, only half cover the coooked fruit with the crumble mix. In the meantime you could prepare the decorative fruits while the crumble-topped fruit is in the oven:

• To make an apple rose, follow the instructions on page 21, then set to one side. Thinly slice the plums and cut out flowers from the flesh using a daisy cutter or similar, and halve the blackberries.

• When the crumble has come out of the oven, decorate the exposed baked fruit with the decorative fresh fruit and serve.

Concorde Cake

I first discovered this dessert when looking for ways to use up egg whites, something I seem to have endless amounts of. It has everything a great dessert should have – richness, texture and surprise with the chocolate mousse and meringue layers hidden beneath shards of chocolate meringue. You will need to make the chocolate mousse in advance, so do plan ahead.

SERVES 8–10
Use 4 baking sheets

CHOCOLATE MOUSSE
200g (7oz) dark chocolate
250g (9oz) milk chocolate
40g (1½oz/3 tbsp) unsalted butter
6 eggs
1 tsp vanilla bean paste (optional)
300ml (10fl oz/1¼ cups) double (heavy) cream

LIGHTER COLOURED CHOCOLATE MERINGUE DISCS & SHARDS
1 lemon wedge
180g (7oz) egg whites
320g (11¼oz/generous 1½ cups) caster (superfine) sugar
40g (1½oz) cocoa powder

DARKER-COLOURED CHOCOLATE SHARDS
1 lemon wedge
100g (3½oz) egg whites
200g (7oz/1 cup) caster (superfine) sugar
60g (2oz) cocoa powder

TO FINISH
250g (9oz) cherries – or seasonal alternatives
1 tbsp caster (superfine) sugar
2 tbsp Kirsch (optional)
icing (powdered) sugar, for dusting

Make the chocolate mousse as instructed on page 110. Transfer to 2 disposable piping (pastry) bags and leave to set in the fridge for at least 4 hours. Preheat the oven to 100°C fan/120°C/240°F/gas ¼–½.

Draw around a 20cm (8 inch) round plate on a sheet of non-stick baking paper to create a template. Repeat once more, then turn both sheets over so that the ink is underneath. Line 2 of the baking sheets with the templates and line the others with unmarked baking paper.

To make the lighter-coloured chocolate meringue, secure the whisk attachment to the mixer and rub a wedge of lemon around the inside of the bowl. Add the egg whites and whisk on a medium speed until soft peaks have formed. Tip the bowl to test if they are ready; if the egg whites slide, whisk for a minute or so longer. Otherwise, turn the mixer to a higher speed and start to add the sugar 1 dessertspoon at a time. When all of the sugar has been added and the meringues are stiff, rub a little between your fingers; if you can feel grains of sugar, whisk for a further 2 minutes, then test again. When smooth, turn the speed to low, add the cocoa powder and whisk until combined and chocolatey.

Transfer the chocolate meringue to a disposable piping (pastry) bag fitted with a plain nozzle (tip) and pipe onto the 2 templates – securing the edges of the baking paper with a little meringue will make this easier. Starting in the middle of each circle, use a steady stream of meringue to create a spiral, piping until the outside of the circle is reached. Don't worry about the discs being neat, they will be covered in chocolate mousse and won't be seen. They do need to be complete though, making them stable for layering, so fill in any gaps as you go. Pipe long straight lengths of meringue onto the remaining baking sheets, using it all up.

Make the darker-coloured chocolate meringue in exactly the same way as the lighter one, but only pipe long straight lengths, using up all of the meringue.

Place all of the baking sheets in the oven and bake for 2 hours until firm and crisp, checking the undersides by lifting them off the paper. If they look slightly gooey or wet, continue to bake until completely dry. Switch off the oven, with the meringues inside until the oven cools. Transfer to an airtight container.

When everything is ready to assemble, wash and stone the cherries, mix with the sugar and Kirsch and set aside.

Lay one of the meringue discs on a serving plate and cover the disc with the chocolate mousse, using one of the bags to pipe out equal-sized chocolate domes. Lay the second meringue disc on top, then repeat with more mousse, moving onto the second bag when needed, but reserving a little.

Break long shards of meringue into various lengths, ranging from 5–8cm (2–3 inches). Spread a little of the remaining mousse onto each meringue shard and use it to adhere each to the outside of the chocolatey layers. Place each one, side by side, alternating between the lighter- and darker-coloured shards until the outside of the cake is covered. Break any remaining lengths of meringue into smaller pieces and use them to top the cake. Finish with a dusting of icing (powdered) sugar, then accompany with the macerated cherries and some cream, adding flowers and a ribbon too if liked. It is important to assemble this dessert close to the time of eating, to retain the crispness of the meringues.

WEEKEND BREAKFAST
& BRUNCH

Homemade Butter

Butter is one of my biggest vices, I really love it. Whether it is being used in baking or cooking, simply spread over toasted crumpets or stirred through mashed potato, butter makes everything better. My Mum used to load everything with butter, maybe that's why I love it so much, she used to practically slice it on toast! Of course I'm not saying to do that, but I do believe that good butter enjoyed moderately is a very special thing indeed.

MAKES 140G (5OZ/⅔ CUP)

300ml (10fl oz/1¼ cups) double (heavy) cream
½ tsp salt – fine table salt or salt crystals, plus extra for sprinkling

Pour the cream into a bowl of a free-standing mixer fitted with the whisk attachment. Whisk on a high speed until the cream splits into liquid (buttermilk) and fat (butterfat) – this will take about 2–3 minutes. Drain off the buttermilk and continue to whisk the butterfat for another minute, aiming to expel as much liquid as possible. Drain again, then add the salt and give a final, yet brief mix.

Lay out a clean piece of muslin (cheesecloth) or a tea towel and transfer the butterfat to the centre. Bring up the sides and squeeze tightly, removing the last drops of buttermilk from the mix. Unwrap and transfer to a sheet of non-stick baking paper sprinkled with some extra salt. Roll the butter into a cylinder and wrap up tightly. Store in the fridge and use within 7 days.

Variation: you can flavour this butter with all kinds of things from seeds to aromats. Or if using for savoury cooking add some garlic, herbs, shallots or chilli and use to baste or cook with.

Lemon Curd

I love lemon curd and use it for many different things, whether simply spread onto toast or drizzled over crêpes, layered between cakes or swirled in to yoghurt. It's also great for enhancing desserts, as it provides little pockets of sharp citrus flavour to balance out any sugary sweetness, enlivening everything from fruit tarts to a pavlova.

MAKES 450G (1LB)

200g (7oz/generous ¾ cup/1¾ sticks) unsalted butter, cubed
200g (7oz/1 cup) caster (superfine) sugar
zest and juice of 3 lemons
5 egg yolks

Set a large heatproof bowl over a pan of simmering water and place the butter, sugar, lemon zest and juice into it. Allow the heat to melt the butter, then stir until the sugar has dissolved. Add the egg yolks and gently whisk everything until all has combined.

With the water still gently simmering below, whisk the mixture continuously for about 10 minutes, or until the curd has thickened enough to coat the back of a spoon. Remove from the heat and sieve into a jug, then pour into sterilized jars. Leave to cool before securing the lids and place in the fridge for at least 4 hours to thicken further.

Strawberry Jam (Jelly)

Imagine looking down at a breakfast of toasted crumpets, butter and jam (jelly)and knowing that you made everything yourself. It's a very satisfying feeling and totally achievable with a bit of forward planning.
The jam (jelly) could also be used to spread between a Victoria Sponge (see page 60) or perhaps used to fill some Doughnuts (see page 100). Whatever its use, the outcome will be delicious, the addition of the star anise adding an edge of complexity.

MAKES 1 X 300ML
(10FL OZ) JAM (JELLY)JAR

600g (21oz) strawberries
400g (14oz/2 cups) jam (jelly)
　sugar
juice of ½ lemon
½ star anise (optional)

Sterilize a suitable jam (jelly) jar and set aside.

Wash and hull the strawberries and gently dry them using kitchen paper – drying the fruit is necessary as any excess water can alter the recipe and the jam(jelly) may not set properly. Halve the berries, then place them in a bowl with the sugar to macerate for at least 2 hours. Macerating the fruit will help the berries stay vibrant in colour and prevent them from breaking down too much during cooking – it will also intensify the strawberry flavour.

If you have a jam (jelly) pan, put the strawberries, and anything that remains in the bowl into it – if not a large pan will do. Squeeze in the lemon juice, add a splash of water and the star anise, if using. Use a wet pastry brush to wash down any sugar crystals that are sticking to the sides of the pan and gently heat until all the sugar has completely dissolved.

Place 2 small plates in the fridge (these are needed to check the jam (jelly) has reached setting point a little later).

Turn up the heat and bring the mixture to a hard boil for 8–10 minutes, or until the temperature on a sugar (candy) or digital thermometer reaches 105°C (221°F). If you don't have a thermometer, remove one of the chilled plates and put a little of the jam (jelly) on it. After 30 seconds, move the jam (jelly) with a finger, making a well – it should wrinkle a little, like jelly (jello), and the gap should stay empty. If the gap floods with juices, setting point hasn't yet been reached, so boil for 2 more minutes then re-test using the other plate.

Once the temperature or setting point has been reached, remove the pan from the heat and leave to cool but not enough that it starts to set. If there seems to be excessive liquid at this point, drain some of this off and discard. Spoon away any impurities that rise to the surface, then leave to sit for 15–20 minutes so that it sets a little. Spoon the jam (jelly) into the sterilized jars, discarding the star anise, cover with some waxed paper and seal airtight. Once the jam (jelly) has been re-opened, store in the fridge.

English Muffins

Homemade English muffins are a great thing. Once you have made your own, I'm sure you will never go back to buying commercially made ones. These are light and soft and are really nothing like the dense ones you can buy in the supermarkets. They make up one part of my favourite of all brunch dishes, Eggs Benedict. They are however just as splendid, simply toasted under a hot grill (broiler) and topped with some homemade Lemon Curd (see page 155) – and My Homemade Butter (see page 155)… of course.

SERVES 12

100ml (3½fl oz/generous ⅓ cup) water
200ml (7fl oz/ generous ¾ cup) milk
30g (1¼oz/2 tbsp) unsalted butter
350g (12oz/2½ cups) strong white bread flour, plus extra for dusting
1 tbsp caster (superfine) sugar
pinch of salt
7g (¼oz) sachet of easy-bake yeast
oil, for greasing
semolina, for sprinkling

Put the water, milk and butter in a small pan, gently heating until the butter melts, then set aside.

Place the flour in the bowl of a free-standing mixer fitted with a dough hook and add the sugar and salt to one side of the bowl and the yeast to the other side. With the mixer running, pour in the tepid milky mixture and mix on a low-medium speed for 10 minutes. The dough will seem wet at first, but should come together nicely after the 10 minutes. If, however, it still seems wet after this time, add a sprinkling of flour and mix again for 2 more minutes. The dough should now be smooth and if pinched between your fingers, shouldn't stick. Place the dough in a lightly oiled bowl and cover tightly with clingfilm (plastic wrap). Leave to rest for about 1½ hours in a warm place until doubled in size, but this time will vary.

Once the dough has doubled, turn out onto a lightly floured surface. Dust the surface with some more flour, then roll out to 1cm (½ inch) thick. Use a 7cm (2¾ inch) cutter to cut out as many muffins as you can – it may help to dip the cutter into flour. Place the muffins on to a sheet of non-stick baking paper, loosely cover with clingfilm (plastic wrap) and leave to rise for 30–40 minutes.

Gently heat a large heavy-based frying pan (skillet) or griddle and moderately sprinkle the surface of the pan with semolina – cooking on top of the semolina will prevent the muffins from sticking and burning. Transfer the muffins to the pan, and leave to slowly cook for about 5 minutes until they are lightly browned and have plumped up. Turn them over with a palette knife and cook on the other side for a few more minutes until equally as golden. The pan may need another sprinkling of the semolina. Once the muffins are cooked on both sides and feel light when lifted, transfer them to a wire rack. Repeat until all of the muffins are cooked.

The muffins now need toasting. Gently pull the muffins apart and toast each half under a medium grill (broiler) until crisp and golden. Top with anything from poached eggs to Lemon Curd (see page 155).

Banana, Pecan & Chocolate Muffins

These muffins are a winner with the kids and can be made really quickly. I like to serve them still warm with a drizzling of maple syrup over the top and some extra banana sliced on the side. You could, however, change the flavourings – raspberries and white chocolate are delicious, or cut out the chocolate and replace with dried fruits, more nuts or even seeds. The method would remain the same, just add the alternatives towards the end of mixing and bake.

MAKES 8 MUFFINS

Use one 12-hole or two 6-hole muffin trays

80g (2¾oz/⅓ cup/¾ stick) unsalted butter

300g (10½oz/2¼ cups) self-raising (self-rising) flour

½ tsp baking powder

100g (3½oz/½ cup) caster (superfine) sugar

220ml (7½fl oz/ scant 1 cup) milk

1 egg

1 tbsp maple syrup, plus extra to finish (optional)

50g (1¾oz/½ cup) milk or dark chocolate, broken into small pieces

50g (1¾oz) pecans, toasted and chopped

100g (3½oz) mashed banana – the riper the better

sugar nibs (optional)

Preheat the oven to 180°C fan/200°C/400°F/gas 6. Place 8 muffin cases into the holes of a muffin tray.

Gently melt the butter in a pan and leave to cool. Sieve together the flour and baking powder, then re-sift into the bowl of a free-standing mixer. Add the sugar and secure the paddle attachment.

Whisk together the milk and the egg, then pour onto the flour and sugar. Mix on a medium speed until everything comes together but do stop the moment that it does so. Add the melted butter and maple syrup, if using, chopped chocolate, pecans and the mashed banana and give everything a quick mix, just enough to combine, then spoon the mixture equally between the muffin cases.

Sprinkle each muffin with some of the sugar nibs, if using, and bake for about 30 minutes. Check for readiness by inserting a skewer into the centre of the muffins – if it comes out clean they are ready; if not quite ready, bake for a further 5 minutes and re-check.

When fully baked, remove the muffins from the oven, spoon over some maple syrup, if using, while still hot, then lift each from the muffin tray and leave to cool a little in their cases before eating.

Plum & Oat Bars

These little flapjack bars will give anyone a much-required energy boost on a morning, or whenever needed throughout the day. The hint of ginger is lovely and warming and works so well with the plums. Mix the flavours to suit your taste or what you have in the kitchen – dried fruits, different nuts and other stone fruits all work well. If you want the bars to keep for longer than two days, it is best to replace the fresh fruit with dried; the retaining moisture in the fresh fruit after baking will turn the bars soft after the second day.

MAKES 12–18 BARS

Use a 30 x 21cm (12 x 8½ inch) baking tin (pan)

150g (5½oz/⅔ cup/1¼ sticks) unsalted butter, plus extra for greasing

50g (1¾oz/¼ cup) light soft brown sugar

10 tbsp golden syrup (light corn syrup)

400g (14oz/4½ cups) rolled oats

pinch of salt

25g (1oz) crystallized (candied) ginger, finely chopped

50g (1¾oz/¼ cup) flaked almonds

50g (1¾oz/ ¼ cup) blanched whole almonds

5 plums (any variety), halved, stoned and cut into 1cm (½ inch) pieces

Preheat the oven to 150°C fan/170°C/325°F/gas 3. Grease and line the baking tin (pan) with non-stick baking paper.

Melt together the butter, sugar and half the syrup, very gently heating until the sugar has completely dissolved. Set aside and leave to cool a little.

Place the oats along with a pinch of salt in a large bowl, stir through the ginger and both the flaked and blanched almonds and make a well in the centre. Pour the syrupy butter into the well and stir together until all is evenly combined. Add the plums, giving a brief mix through, then spoon the mixture into the lined tin (pan). Press the mixture down to create an even layer, reaching right to the corners of the tin (pan). Bake for 30 minutes.

Meanwhile, gently heat the remaining syrup in a small pan. After the 30 minutes baking, drizzle the molten syrup over the surface of the oats and return the tin (pan) to the oven to bake for a further 20 minutes.

Turn the oven down to 120°C fan/140°C/275°F/gas 1 and bake for about 30 minutes, or until hardened.

Leave in the tin (pan) until cooled and crisp, then cut into suitable bar-sized portions.

Remove and store in an airtight container, storing each slice between layers of non-stick baking paper.

Heart-shaped Churros

Homemade churros are an absolute treat and they tend to be loved by all – children and adults alike. We try and make a batch during the school holidays when they are enjoyed as a mid-morning snack. They also make for a quirky and fun dessert, dipped into chocolate sauce and served with an extra pot of sprinkles for the kids. It's best to make the chocolate sauce first so that you can eat the churros as soon as they have been fried.

SERVES 6

75g (2¾oz/⅓ cup/¾ stick)
  unsalted butter
250ml (9fl oz/generous
  1 cup) water
150g (5½oz/generous 1 cup)
  plain (all-purpose) flour
pinch of salt
3 eggs
1 litre (33¾fl oz/4 ¼ cups
  plus 3 tbsp) sunflower or
  vegetable oil, for frying

COATING
100g (3½oz/½ cup) caster
  (superfine) sugar
1 tsp ground spices, such
  as cinnamon or allspice
  (optional)
sprinkles (optional)

CHOCOLATE SAUCE
50g (1¾oz) dark chocolate,
  broken into small pieces
50g (1¾oz) milk chocolate,
  broken into small pieces
1 tbsp golden syrup (light
  corn syrup)
50g (1¾oz/3½ tbsp) unsalted
  butter, chilled and cubed
180ml (6fl oz/¾ cup) double
  (heavy) cream

To make the chocolate sauce, place the chocolate in a heatproof bowl set on top of a pan of simmering water. Add the syrup and butter and allow the heat to gently melt everything. Once melted, stir everything together to fully combine, then add the cream in 3 stages, mixing well with each addition. Once all of the cream has been added and the mixture is both smooth and glossy, remove from the heat and transfer to a bowl.

To make the churros paste, add the butter and water to a large pan and bring the water to the boil, melting the butter as it does so. Mix the flour and salt together and add this to the pan, stirring well until the flour and water form a stiff paste. Remove from the heat and leave to cool for 10 minutes, beating occasionally to aid the cooling process.

When suitably cooled, beat the eggs together in a jug, then add a little at a time to the flour paste – mixing well between each addition. It may seem like the egg will not combine at first, but it will. Once all of the eggs are fully combined and your paste is thick and glossy, transfer it to a disposable piping (pastry) bag fitted with a star nozzle (tip).

Make the coating by mixing the sugar together with the ground spices (if using) and spread onto a large plate or tray and set aside.

If using a deep fat fryer, set the temperature to 180°C/350°F; if heating the oil in a pan carefully bring the oil to temperature. Check with a digital thermometer or test by dropping a little of the batter in to the oil – if hot enough, the batter should immediately start to sizzle.

The churros paste can be piped directly into the oil by squeezing the bag and snipping off lengths with some scissors. If you would like to make hearts, pipe the shapes out onto individual pieces of non-stick baking paper. Cooking in batches, carefully drop the churros (paper and all) into the hot oil. As soon as the churros start to cook, the paper will slip away and the piped shape will remain. The paper can then be removed with tongs. Fry for 2–3 minutes, turning once. The batter will turn golden and the exterior will be crisp when ready. Remove from the oil, allowing any excess oil to drip away, then immediately toss in the spiced sugar. Leave to cool for a few minutes before enjoying with the chocolate sauce and sprinkles, if using.

American-style Pancakes

These pancakes are lovely and light in texture and are so delicious when fried in bubbling, brown butter, they only take a few minutes to cook. Simply pour over some maple syrup for a quick breakfast, or if time allows, be a little more indulgent. You could top them with anything from bacon and eggs to thick yoghurt and fruit, honey and candied nuts or even some chocolate sauce. My Mum always said 'you should breakfast like a king,' and when time is on my side, it is something I try and adhere to, especially at the weekends. You can prepare this batter the night before as it will keep well in the fridge. Great if you tend to be in a bit of rush in the morning.

MAKES 8–10 PANCAKES

40g (1½oz/3 tbsp) unsalted
  butter
200g (7oz/1½ cups) plain
  (all-purpose) flour
1 tsp baking powder
2 tbsp caster (superfine) sugar
pinch of salt
2 eggs
300ml (10fl oz/1¼ cups) milk
oil and butter, for frying

TO FINISH
selection of seasonal fruits
maple syrup

Melt the butter in a small pan and set aside. Sieve the flour and baking powder into a large bowl, then repeat – doing so will incorporate the baking powder more evenly throughout the flour. Add the sugar and salt and make a well in the centre. Separate the eggs, adding the yolks to the milk and putting the whites in a separate bowl. Give the milk and yolks a good mix, then gradually pour into the flour bowl, whisking as you do so. Gradually draw in more of the flour until all of the flour has been combined and you have a smooth and lump-free batter. Add the melted butter and combine completely.

Whisk the egg whites until they form soft peaks. Test by tilting the bowl to one side – if the egg whites slide, whisk them some more; if they hold, they're ready. Gently fold one-third of the whites into the pancake batter, being as light handed as you can, then fold in the rest. You don't want to lose all of those air bubbles that you have taken time and energy to whisk up.

Heat a non-stick mini frying pan (skillet) over a medium heat, add a little oil and a knob of butter and leave to melt. When the butter starts to go frothy, spoon in a generous tablespoon of the batter per pancake and even out, swirling the pan until the batter reaches the edges. Cook for about 1 minute, turning when air bubbles appear on the surface of the batter. Gently flip over using a palette knife and cook on the other side for another minute. Rest on kitchen paper and repeat until all of the batter has been used, keeping the already cooked pancakes warm as you do so.

Stack a few pancakes per person on a warmed plate and top with some fresh fruit and finish by drizzling over a generous glug of maple syrup.

Crumpets

If I had to describe crumpets in a short, sharp sentence, it would be 'butter's best friend'. I love butter, it's my Mother's doing, her food was always loaded with it. Toasted items came with a thick slice of butter on top, and crumpets in particular were always served dripping with the stuff! I do the same now, much to a raised eyebrow from my husband. It is definitely my biggest vice, my not-so guilty pleasure. I like to serve these crumpets simply spread with some Homemade Butter (see page 155), but they can be topped with anything that takes your fancy, from fruit compôtes to honey-scented yoghurt.

MAKES 6 CRUMPETS

150ml (5fl oz/scant ⅔ cup) milk

150ml (5fl oz/scant ⅔ cup) water

200g (7oz/scant 1½ cups) strong white bread flour

1 tsp salt

1 tsp bicarbonate of (baking) soda

1 tsp caster (superfine) sugar

½ tsp easy-bake dried yeast

Combine the milk and water in a pan, gently warm through and set to one side. In a large bowl, sieve the flour, add the salt, bicarbonate of (baking) soda and sugar and make a well in the centre. Add the yeast to the well, then slowly pour in the warmed liquid, whisking as you do so, drawing in the flour a little at a time until it has all been combined and a smooth, lump-free batter remains. Cover the bowl with clingfilm (plastic wrap) and leave to develop and prove for at least 1 hour or until the batter has gained in volume and bubbles appear on the surface. The batter can be made up to 8 hours in advance and doing so will give a stronger flavour to the finished product.

Set a non-stick mini frying pan (skillet) – the ones you fry eggs in – over a very low heat. Spoon some of the batter into the pan and gently dry fry for a few minutes, until the holes appear and the top of the crumpet sets. Remove from the pan, refilling with more batter, frying until all of the batter has been used.

Once the crumpets have been cooked on the stove top, they can be toasted. I recommend doing so underneath a grill (broiler) as the bottoms may burn in a toaster, depending on how much colour they have taken on during the initial cooking.

Once toasted, spread with your favourite topping and enjoy hot.

Crêpes with Citrus Salad

When we were young, Mum only ever made us crêpes (or pancakes as we call them) on Shrove Tuesday. To be fed pancakes for dinner, even if it was just once a year, was such a treat! I would have condensed milk drizzled over mine! Even now, the slightest taste of condensed milk takes me back to childhood in a flash. I'm not suggesting you top your crêpes with condensed milk, but here is a lovely brunch dish that I am sure you will enjoy. It is a take on the classic French dessert, crêpes Suzette, just without the addition of any alcohol or the faff of flambéing. That said, a nice glass of Bucks Fizz would be a perfect accompaniment to this, special occasion or not.

SERVES 4

CREPES (MAKES 8)
200g (7oz/1½ cups) plain
  (all-purpose) flour
pinch of salt
1 tbsp caster (superfine) sugar
3 eggs
300ml (10fl oz/1¼ cups) milk
vegetable oil, for frying

ORANGE SYRUP
3 tbsp caster (superfine) sugar
250ml (9fl oz/generous
  1 cup) freshly squeezed
  orange juice (about 3 large
  oranges)
zest of 1 orange
50g (1¾oz/3½ tbsp) unsalted
  butter, cubed

OPTIONAL TOPPINGS
selection of oranges (Navel,
  clementine, blood oranges),
  segmented
plain yoghurt
fresh mint – smaller leaves
  picked

Prepare the crêpe batter by placing the flour, salt and sugar in a large bowl, making a well in the centre. Mix the eggs with the milk in a separate bowl or jug, then slowly pour this into the well, whisking as you do so, gradually bringing in more of the flour. Keep whisking until all of the milk mixture has been added and the batter is smooth. The batter should be lump free, but if not, you can always pass it through a sieve.

Heat a crêpe pan (or large non-stick frying pan/skillet) and add a little oil, wiping away any excess with a piece of kitchen paper. When the pan is hot, add a ladleful of batter, tilting and swirling the pan until all of the surface has been covered. Pour any spare batter back into the bowl – this will ensure you get lovely thin crêpes. Fry for 1–2 minutes, then turn or flip over and fry on the other side. The crêpes should be slightly golden. Repeat until all of the batter has been used. Fold the crêpes into quarters and stack on a plate until later.

Make the orange syrup. Put the sugar and a splash of water in a large frying pan (skillet) , swirling the pan until the sugar dissolves. Place over a medium heat and let the sugar solution bubble until a golden caramel has been reached (see tips on making caramel on page 131). Add a little of the orange juice – it will steam and spit a little, so do be careful. Add the rest of the juice and let the caramel melt back into the liquid. Add the orange zest, then the butter, just a little at a time, giving it all a whisk to combine. Simmer a little and let the sauce thicken slightly.

Add the folded crêpes to the pan, spooning over the orange syrup. Warm through for a couple of minutes, then serve on warmed plates, pouring over any remaining syrup. Top with the citrus segments, add a spoonful of yoghurt and sprinkle over some mint leaves.

Tip: to prepare the fruit segments, remove the skin and pith with a sharp knife, trying not to take any of the fruit with it. Cut out the citrus flesh from each segment and keep to one side until needed.

Equipment & Suppliers

Free-standing mixer – My most treasured piece of kitchen equipment and one that I use almost every day. If you don't have one already and tend to bake often, I would recommend investing in one. Not only will it save you time but it will save you a lot of effort too. Prices range considerably, so do find the best one for your budget. What is important is to check that the one you choose has a decent motor and includes all of the attachments that you will need.

Cake tins, baking sheets and tart tins (pans) – I have a vast selection of good-quality bakeware, which I have collected over the years. Each item is still as good as the day it was bought. There are so many ranges available and it is worth paying the extra few pounds for ones that are well made and have a non-stick coating.

Mixing bowls – You can never have enough! Or it certainly seems that way when I bake.

Utensils – A selection of silicone spatulas, a balloon whisk a plastic scraper, palette knives, straight and cranked, a Swiss-style vegetable peeler and a sharp knife are amongst my most used utensils; all making the job in hand easier and contributing to a neater finish. None of these items needs to be expensive. Oh… and a fine sieve would be handy too.

Oven thermometers – Essential in my opinion. It can be quite surprising how different the thermometer will read to that of the oven dial – even in a new oven. I have experience of this, and after wondering why my bakes weren't cooking in time, off I set to buy a thermometer with the temperature difference being adjusted the problem was then easily resolved.

Disposable piping (pastry) bags and a selection of piping nozzles (tips) – The disposable bags are great to have to hand, I always have a roll tucked away so I can decorate cakes or pipe meringues if I get the urge.

Non-stick baking paper – The white-silicone coated variety, indispensable – I use metres (yards) of the stuff!

STOCKISTS

UK

Divertimenti
www.divertimenti.co.uk

John Lewis
www.johnlewis.com

Kitchen Aid
www.kitchenaid.com

Lakeland
www.lakeland.co.uk

Steamer Trading
www.steamer.co.uk

Timeless Homes & Gifts
www.timelesshomesandgifts.co.uk

US

Crate and Barrel
www.crateandbarrel.com

Sur La Table
www.surlatable.com

Williams Sonoma
Www.williams-sonoma.com

AUSTRALIA

Everten
www.everten.com.au

Kitchen Warehouse
www.kitchenwarehouse.com.au

Robins Kitchen
www.robinskitchen.com.au

Index

Acknowledgements

Working on this book has been emotional to say the least. Excitement, exhaustion, joy, admiration, pride, love and apprehension, highs and lows, it has certainly been an adventure and a learning curve! Of all the emotions, there is one that will remain long after this book has gone to print: gratitude… unwavering gratitude to all of those who have helped me along the way – both professionally and personally. From laughter through to panic and back again we've been through it all together! Each and every one of you has helped me to get through this and each and everyone one of you is a part of these pages.

Firstly, I would like to thank Jo, my editor, for keeping me on track and making this book such a pleasure to write and to work on. Thank you so much for making this happen. Never did I imagine that I would write a cookbook. Rachel, thank you for making every page so beautiful. Your dedication, understanding and patience will never be forgotten! Special thanks to Jacqui for believing in me and trusting a complete novice to deliver. Continuing thanks to all of those behind the scenes at Quarto Books, the team is much bigger than it seems and I thank you all.

Lisa, you have captured everything so beautifully, I am so happy that it was you. Thanks to you and Dom for making my first cookbook such a great experience to shoot… for putting up with my bad taste in 80s music and for embracing MJ, I loved it. It has been an absolute pleasure to work with you and to learn so much along the way.

I had some great help leading up to and during the photo shoots. Thank you to Lucy Harvey for going the extra mile. Liz you moved around my kitchen like a 20-year-old, thank you so much for answering my call of help; what an amazing lady you are. And enormous thanks go out to Andy Stacey, a true life-saver if ever there was one. Thank you from the bottom of my heart, you are a true gent and a great friend and I shall remember those kitchen days with great fondness.

Cara, my beautiful niece: thank you so much for being there, you made me so proud to be your aunty… and, you make the best coffees ever! I love you loads x.

Thanks also to Vicki, who found herself roped in to help after we'd only been reacquainted for 5 minutes. It was great having you on board.

I have some amazing friends. Honestly a day never passes without me realizing how lucky I am. I have been given encouragement and support from so many of you, I just wish I had enough pages to thank you all individually; unfortunately I haven't, but please know I am very grateful to you all, from the taste testers to the prop providers, you're amazing, each and every one of you. Special thanks are needed for those that helped me with the children, those that came to my aid without hesitation: Rachael, Sam and Nicola, I am so indebted to you all. To my wonderful neighbours Tony and Irene, for helping me with the boys and for letting me raid those treasure troves of crockery, you're the best.

Then there is Marilyn, who when I was burned out and fading, reignited the spark. I shall never forget it Buffet… I love you dearly. Beautiful, courageous Carla, it was such an honour to call you my friend. How I will miss you.

Enormous amounts of love and thanks go out to my family. I love you all very much, thank you all for your continued support throughout this project. Special thanks to both my Dad and my Stepdad Gerry, I am a much stronger person because of you. To Jonah, for listening tirelessly to my ramblings on food and for eating so much cake when really you'd had enough of all things gluten! I love you babe, thank you for your endless patience. A special shout out to my three gorgeous boys: Evan, Oscar and Myles, you all fill my heart with so much love and pride and in return that love inspires me daily. To my Mum who is forever in my heart and guides me in all that I do. I love you so, so much Mamma, I just hope that in your heart you still know it.

Finally, a HUGE thank you to the Instagram community. To have you all on board bowls me over. I feel like I have friends the world over and it's a very special thing indeed. Thank you for your continued support, words of encouragement and for the love that you send me and my Mum daily. You are amazing, all of you x